Allotment
Gardening

Allotment Gardening

An Organic Guide for Beginners

Susan Berger

with drawings by Jennifer Johnson
and photographs by Nicola Browne

Green Books

First published in 2005
by Green Books Ltd
Foxhole, Dartington
Totnes, Devon TQ9 6EB

Cover design by Rick Lawrence
samskara@onetel.com

Illustrations © Jennifer Johnson

Photographs © Nicola Browne
www.nicolabrowne.co.uk

Text printed on Five Seasons Stone-White 100% recycled paper
Covers made from 80% recycled fibres

Printed and bound by MPG Books Ltd, Bodmin, Cornwall

British Library Cataloguing in Publication Data
available on request

ISBN 1 903998 54 9

Contents

To Tom Hardwick, whose Oxford allotment should
prove the perfect antidote to academic life.

Acknowledgements

I would like to thank my editor Amanda Cuthbert at Green Books, whose clarity and patience kept me on track and focused just when I needed it most; John Elford, whose enthusiasm and support for the book was there from day one; and Jennifer Johnson for her delightful drawings.

Also Geoff Stokes from the National Society of Allotment and Leisure Gardens who patiently answered endless queries about allotment rules and regulations, and Jackie Gear at HDRA for her willingness to confirm questions about organic practice.

My thanks too go to Sonia Ashmore, whose abundant allotment inspired me to become an allotment gardener, and I particularly want to thank Karena Batstone, who encouraged me to write the book in the first place, and Charlotte Packer who then kept reminding me that I could do it.

Part One

GETTING STARTED

Introduction

The allotment today is a stress-free oasis offering a chance for the creativity, calm and pleasure that gardening in the fresh air can bring—and it's cheaper than joining a gym! The aim of this book is to help you get the most from your allotment by making the best use of your time on site. It can be a formidable challenge when you first take it on, especially if your only gardening experience has been to keep a pot of supermarket herbs going for a week or two. But it's a satisfying challenge working in the fresh air, placing a tiny seed in the ground and bringing the results to the table a few months later.

Allotment gardening is a fantastic opportunity to grow the sort of food you love to eat, and with this in mind there are some simple recipes in the A-Z lists in Part Two. You need never again spend a fortune on those pre-packed bags of salad leaves: instead you can sow a packet of seeds for the cost of one bag, and be picking leaves twice a week for the whole summer. And potatoes! Those waxy salad potatoes beloved of the French are often the most expensive to buy, and all potatoes are easy to grow. The same can be said for dwarf French beans, red onions, beetroot, Swiss chard, raspberries, sugar snap peas and rocket—the ingredients for a cook's paradise. Imagine sharing a mid-summer supper of tortilla cooked slowly with allotment potatoes and red onions, accompanied by freshly picked salad leaves and Cos lettuce tossed in a garlicky dressing. You may even get a late crop of asparagus to coincide with a bowl of early strawberries. Above all else, you will know that the produce you are eating is as fresh as is humanly possible and entirely free of chemicals.

The produce chosen for the book is based on two considerations. First it is easy to grow, and second it is high in flavour. In the last forty years, multi-nationals have bought up large seed companies within the countries of the European Union. A 'Common Catalogue' makes it illegal for commercial growers to sell any vegetable not on their country's national list. Seed suppliers stopped producing many extremely flavoursome and pest-resistant old varieties because there was no demand from commercial growers. However, several companies have reintroduced these old varieties for the amateur gardener. They can be found in many of the seed catalogues listed at the back of the book. In 1975 The Henry Doubleday Research Organisation set up the Heritage Seed Library to promote and conserve genetic diversity in vegetable crops. Membership entitles you to six packets of vegetable seeds free annually, plus seed-saving guidelines.

Today we want the least possible chemical intervention in our food and we understand the benefits of fresh air and exercise. These factors may explain the rise in popularity in allotment gardening and reflect the diversity of gardeners renting allotments. On a site in Bristol, retired men and women include an eighty-year-old who has a rent-free plot—a concession to honour the fact he has been gardening there for over fifty years. Despite having had major heart surgery, he cycles in most days. Other allotment holders on the same site include students, a docker, a university professor, a novelist, a herbalist, shopkeepers, teachers, single parents, families and a huge variety of age groups and nationalities. Ruth, a Polish woman with a long grey plait down to her waist, grows bucketfuls of beetroot. Tom, an Irishman, mostly grows potatoes for his friends and family. Each plot varies in its orderliness. Some are immaculate, a weed-free series of eight raised beds separated by firm paths of compacted earth. Others are more chaotic, but nonetheless productive.

HISTORY

The benefit of growing your own food has long been recognized as a means of improving the quality of people's lives. In the mid-19th century, people throughout Europe were flocking from country to town to find work in the industrialized areas. Conditions were far from ideal. Overcrowded working and living space combined with poor nutrition resulted in ill health and subsequent unemployment. In 1830 Germany was the first country to set up 'gardens for the poor', offering a chance of self-sufficiency and physical activity in the open air. Many of the migrants from the country had grown vegetables in the past and were more than willing to get their hands in the soil again. In 1869 Schrebergartens (allotments) were developed in 100 sites throughout Germany. By the 1900s, workers' organizations, factory owners and local authorities combined to provide Kleingarten, the first chalet-gardens where families could spend weekends away from the polluted cities. These spread to other parts of Europe, and were known as 'summer-house gardens' in Holland and 'garden colonies' in Denmark. The Danish model inspired the Swedish allotment movement, which was founded in 1909. This 'second home' culture is prominent throughout Scandinavia today, with many owners growing produce and flowers, and all demonstrating the benefit of time spent in the fresh air.

The history of the British allotment can be traced back to the feudal system and the steady loss of common land from the 16th century onwards. By 1818, 5 million acres of formerly open land had been enclosed by Acts of Parliament, denying those without land any means of growing their own food. As in the rest of Europe, poverty and disease were widespread by the mid-19th century. In an attempt to reduce poverty, and under pressure from a small number of landowners who realized too much common land had been enclosed, the government passed the General Enclosure Act of 1845 to provide 'field gardens' for the labouring poor. The *Penny Magazine* in the same year interpreted motives for the act as sanctimonious rather than benevolent:

"The object in making such allotments is moral rather than economic: the cultivation of a few vegetables and flowers is a pleasing occupation and has a tendency to keep a man at home and from the ale house."

This lack of benevolence soon turned allotments into a political issue, and by the beginning of the 20th century, parliamentary seats were fought over them. The Small Holdings and Allotments Act of 1908 made it the responsibility of local authorities to provide allotments in town and country on the demand of four people or more. During the First World War, a dependency on home-grown produce increased the number of allotments to one and a quarter million. Widespread unemployment in the 1920s and 30s kept them going, and by the Second World War they had increased in number to one million four hundred. From the 1950s, the standard of living steadily increased and the popularity of the allotment began to diminish. Acts of

Parliament have never guaranteed their survival, and many sites were developed for housing. The National Society of Allotment and Leisure Gardeners says that whilst allotments are popular again, they are only safe from development when used to capacity. In order to help preserve them, the NSALG promotes the self-management of sites and offers guidelines on how to set up committees. All tenants are issued with an information pack outlining the rules and regulations on allotments.

GO ORGANIC!

This book places an emphasis on ground preparation and soil fertility. Organic gardening undoubtedly involves more labour than chemically aided gardening, but the reward of eating produce untainted by chemicals far outweighs the extra effort. Organic gardening is not difficult, and with practice will set you up with the best gardening skills for life. Follow chapters 4, 5 & 6 carefully, and everything you plant will reward your time spent on the allotment. On pages 54–62 there is a month-by-month calendar, which will keep you on schedule for the tasks that ensure a year-round supply of produce.

HOW MUCH TIME WILL I NEED?

Keeping up a plot can be demanding on your time, especially through spring and summer. In these six months, two hours twice a week plus four hours at the weekends is the sort of commitment needed. For the rest of the year the pace slows down, and two hours a week in autumn and winter should keep you on top of things. A pride in the appearance of the plot and a determination not to lose control of the weeds usually dictates the time you spend on site.

CHILDREN

Your allotment can become a magical place for children. It may be the only space they have to get their hands in the soil. The experience of eating the vegetables they themselves have helped to grow can help to break bad eating habits. More than anything, it offers them the opportunity to develop a respect for nature. Start by helping them dig a hole in the corner of the plot big enough to take a plastic washing-up bowl. Fill it with water and allow grass to grow around it, then watch for pond life. If you can find some frog spawn, your children will learn that the more frogs you attract the less the crops are damaged by slugs, and the less need there is for intervention with pesticides.

Children may like to keep rabbits and hens on an allotment, but avoid cockerels—they are considered too noisy. Permission from your local authority will depend on the suitability of the site, and you will be responsible for funding and building secure pens.

CHOOSING YOUR ALLOTMENT

To rent an allotment, phone your local authority or contact The National Society of Allotment & Leisure Gardens (see address at end of book). You may be put on a waiting list, so the sooner you contact them the better.

The standard size of a plot in the UK is 250 sq. metres. Rents vary around the country and are at the discretion of the local authority. Rural ones can cost as little as £5 per year, in the city charges range from £15 to £60. The most expensive is still less than a £1.50 a week to rent.

If your spare time is limited, consider sharing the allotment with a friend. You can divide the plot in two or share the workload. Bear the following points in mind when assessing the site:

- Try to avoid renting a plot that involves long car journeys from your home.
- Assure yourself that there are enthusiastic people renting round you. Weeds can flourish on unattended plots and will freely seed on cultivated ground. Check as best you can that your neighbour won't be using inorganic pest control and weedkillers.
- Ask what the soil condition is like, or confirm that it's fertile from what you see growing.
- Check that there is good security: a padlocked outer gate is essential wherever you live.
- Make sure there is an adequate water supply such as a tap. It is not statutory but most sites have one shared between several plots.
- Ideally there should be a lockable shed for each plot, and most local authorities provide them. You will be allowed to erect one on bare earth; no concrete foundations are allowed.
- Establish who is responsible for maintaining hedges or fences round the actual site. The path between each plot is usually the joint responsibility of you and your neighbour.

Chapter 1

Tools of the Trade

The following basic tools are what you will need to get started. You can acquire additional equipment as time goes on. Car boot sales, auctions and charity shops are a good source for second-hand gardening equipment.

GARDEN TOOLS

Fork & Spade
Buy stainless-steel types, as they don't rust and are easy to clean. Good DIY stores sell their own brands at reasonable prices. Compare the balance and weight of the different types before you purchase. Most have strong polypropylene plastic shafts that keep them lightweight, while the stainless-steel body makes them strong enough to cope with the heaviest soil.

Hoe
The Dutch hoe has a D-shaped blade, 10–17 cm wide, which is attached to a long shaft. It is useful for all general surface hoeing. To avoid backbreaking stooping, make sure you buy the correct length handle. As a rule, the top of the handle should be level with your ear when the hoe is vertical on the ground.

An onion hoe is a small, swan-neck hoe on a short handle (see pages 47–51 on *Cultivation*).

Rake
A rake is essential for levelling the ground and preparing seedbeds. Most suitable are the ones with metal heads with 10 or 12 short, wide rounded teeth. These are available with strong plastic shafts.

Trowel
A trowel is useful for making small holes into which seedlings can be transplanted. Narrow blades are more useful than broad ones for this. Some have gauges stamped on them for measuring soil depth and are helpful when planting onion sets and garlic.

Hand Fork
This is useful for loosening weeds around established plants.

Bucket
It's always helpful to have a couple of buckets on site when you are working. Use them for transporting small tools and for weeding and cropping.

Watering Can
Many local authorities forbid the use of hoses on allotments so you will find two 7–9 litre capacity cans the fastest way to water your crops. Plastic cans are lighter than galvanized aluminium, and it is helpful to have a detachable rose spray for gently watering very new seedlings.

Plastic Screw-top Spray
Keep a 2–litre spray in the shed with a washing-up liquid mixture ready to use against aphids.

Twine and Skewers
Keep a large ball of gardener's twine and a couple of skewers on site to make straight lines across your plot as a guide when sowing. Use twine to tie climbing plants to supporting canes.

Labels
Buy an economy packet of plastic labels or make your own out of the lids of ice cream containers or discarded lolly sticks. You will need a chinagraph pencil or waterproof pen to write on them.

Sharp Knife
This can be particularly useful for cropping courgettes and marrows, or for slicing the tops off empty plastic water bottles to make cloches for small seedlings.

Scissors
These are good for cutting herbs, salad leaves and flowers.

Refuse Bin

Buy a large dustbin to store material that is too tough to compost.

Wheelbarrow

This is essential if you have lots of clearing and fertilizing to do.

Additional Equipment

The following equipment is very useful for extending the growing season and protecting plants against pests.

Cloches

These are small, moveable units made of plastic or glass, designed to protect crops against frosts.

Cold Frames

These are bottomless boxes with sloping see-through lids that are generally more substantial than cloches and also protect plants from frost.

Horticultural Fleece

This is a spun fibre, like cheesecloth, and can be draped over plants as protection against aphids. Biodegradable fleece is available.

Polytunnels

These are made of lightweight polythene film laid over wire hoops.

Mesh or Netting

This is sold by the metre and available in various sizes. A 2.5 cm mesh is useful for supporting peas or beans, and it makes a good slug deterrent when used to cover newly sown ground.

Mulch Materials

Old carpet, cardboard, pebbles, gravel, well-rotted compost, bark chippings, leaf mould and straw make excellent inexpensive mulches. Round them up if you find them being thrown away and store on site for future use.

Black sheet polypropylene

Useful as this is on large areas, it will inevitably end up in landfill at some stage, so choose biodegradable materials wherever you can. Sometimes known as silage sheet, it is sold by the metre in garden centres. It can be used for weed control, mulching or covering paths.

OTHER USEFUL ITEMS

Airtight Tin
An airtight container for tea bags, powdered milk and matches is useful. You can also store seed packets in a tin to keep them dry and out of the reach of mice.

Containers
Save carrier bags and plastic containers—they can be useful for picking. Save yoghurt pots and butter containers for sowing seeds—you will need to make holes in the bottom.

Fold-up Chair
A lightweight picnic chair is great for the tea break.

Primus Stove
A small primus stove is useful for boiling water for tea. Alternatively take a flask.

Waterproof Jacket
Keep a rainproof jacket and a pair of sunglasses in the shed so you are prepared for all weathers.

Wood
A plank of wood, minimum size 30 cms wide x 1.50 metres long is useful for standing on when you want to plant in winter or wet weather. Dispersing your weight across its length will prevent damage to the soil surface. A 2 metre long x 10 cms wide batten marked up with a waterproof pen every 10 cm is really useful for spacing plants as you put them in the ground.

Chapter 2

Planning the Site

You have your allotment, and it's your first day on site. The plot looks bigger than you imagined and rather overwhelming now that it's yours. You look around: everyone else is busy, you don't know where to begin, and you probably feel somewhat terrified. This chapter will help you to get started.

THINGS TO THINK ABOUT
BEFORE YOU START

The simplest way to use your allotment is to create four main beds and rotate the contents over four years (see pages 20–22 on *Crop Rotation*). In addition you may want to grow fruit, herbs and asparagus which all require permanent beds.

If you are sharing your allotment, you will only be working half the plot. Making permanent beds will reduce the size of your four crop rotation beds, which will be further reduced by paths. So if you are sharing your plot, it may be necessary to make just two rotation beds. Then the golden rule is to rotate root crops one year with 'above ground' crops the next, and vice versa.

Fruit

You may have an established fruit bed on the plot—if not, decide whether you want to make one. Soft fruit such as rhubarb, gooseberries, currants and raspberries are easy to grow but will take two or three years to establish, so it is worth planting these as soon as possible. These fruit freeze well, so once you've eaten enough summer puddings, gooseberry fool and blackcurrant tarts you can freeze any surplus for winter treats. All are tolerant of some shade (worth bearing in mind at the planning stage).

Strawberries don't freeze well and take up quite a lot of ground, so decide whether it's worth it for those two weeks of delicious fruits mid-summer.

Allotments can be exposed to weather extremes such as high winds or baking sunshine, and raspberries will provide useful windbreaks. Look at the layout on other plots and talk to your neighbours for advice on positioning your soft fruit bed.

Herbs
If you use lots of herbs and have no garden, then plan a small permanent bed in the sunniest aspect. Two plants each of perennial rosemary, mint, oregano, marjoram, sage, tarragon and thyme should be enough for keen cooks, and can be fitted in after the four main beds. If you have a garden, you may prefer to grow herbs at home. Annual herbs such as parsley, dill, coriander and chives can be sown in rows across the allotment beds.

Asparagus
You may want to make a permanent space for asparagus. A bed will remain productive for twenty years or more, so it is worth the initial investment—even in season, asparagus is expensive to buy.

Flowers
Flowers play an important role in organic gardening, attracting beneficial insects to the vegetable plot. In Part Two you will find a list of flowers traditionally grown as companion plants that are known to help keep crops healthy. You can sow these next to or close to the crops that suffer most from aphid attack—largely the bean and brassica families. And if you regularly buy flowers for your home, leave an area free for several rows of flowers for cutting, and save a fortune at the florist. Most annual flowers tolerate some shade, and all will benefit from shelter.

Compost Bins
You will need at least two of these. They can be positioned in part shade, but decomposition is faster in the sun. Make sure there is easy access with a wheelbarrow.

Water Butts
Position a water butt or two near the shed to catch rainwater from the roof. Place high up on bricks so that a can will fit on the ground under the tap. Rain tanks are now available made from recycled plastic (see pages 154–155, *Useful Addresses.*)

PLANNING TIPS

Plan on paper first!

Draw the plot on a piece of paper by eye, making it roughly to scale. Mark on existing fruit and herb beds if any, and the site of the shed, water butt and compost bins. Alternatively, measure the entire plot with a tape measure and transfer to paper using a scale rule.

The remnants of old beds may be apparent under all the weed growth; if they are, and if the paths between them are still identifiable, you can clear and use them.

If the plot is empty, decide where you will make the fruit, herb and cut flower beds and the area for compost bins. Make a note on your paper plan then divide the remainder to create four equal beds with paths running between them (see pages 20–22, *Crop Rotation*). You may also find it necessary to make narrow paths within these four beds, but they will evolve spontaneously when you plant.

Sloping sites: Some plots on steeply sloping sites have been terraced, and these should be visible under the weeds and brambles. Stick to the existing terracing, as you might not want to get into digging and levelling new ones!

Transfer the Plan to your Site

Transfer the plan by using bamboo canes and a tape measure to define all the beds and the paths between. Use skewers and twine within the canes to get the lines straight—you'll be amazed how out of line you can go.

If the ground is covered in brambles you'll need to clear these first (see pages 23–26). If the ground is simply overgrown with weeds, mark out the paths from your paper plan and make them first to avoid spending time and energy digging and weeding soil that will be a simple walkway.

Paths

Paths are made of compacted earth, achieved by covering and thereby starving the ground of oxygen and rainfall. Laying a run of cardboard across the plot (the sort you get with flat-pack furniture), cut to the width of the path, is a fast way to compact the soil. The more you walk on it, the harder the soil becomes. The cardboard will gradually disintegrate, but not before a firm path is established. The same results can be achieved with a run of discarded stair carpet, but put the underside uppermost: a row of swirly orange Axminsters can detract from the simple beauty of rows of healthy vegetables! Only use carpets with a biodegradable hessian backing. (As a last resort, cover the paths with heavy-duty, black plastic cut to size and dug in at the edges.)

Don't be tempted to make grass paths. You will spend all your time mowing and edging, and the grass will encroach on the growing area in no time at all. However, if your allotment already has grass paths established, then leave them and use a lawn mower to keep them trim. With the paths in place you will then begin to feel you're making progress and can work on the beds in a systematic way.

Chapter 3

Crop Rotation

Many people, when they first get an allotment, are so keen to start sowing that they ignore the principles of crop rotation. They clear some ground, sow and plant, and gradually work their way up the plot. This is fine for a year or two: you'll probably get good results, and it's a great way to learn what crops are easy and what crops need most attention. But in the long term you'll get better results for your efforts if you grow certain crops on a different area of ground each year. The aim is to reduce the build-up of diseases and thus reduce the need to use chemicals. In addition to this, certain vegetables add nutrients to the soil, thereby improving the ground for the next crop.

There are four family groups of vegetables to rotate: onions and roots, potatoes, brassicas and legumes. Using this method of crop rotation you need only apply manure to a quarter of the ground each year, to the site where the hungriest feeders—the brassicas—are planted. The grouping is also convenient; for example, onion and root vegetables will survive with little water, and are separate from legumes that require regular watering. And members of the brassica family grown together can be covered with a horticultural fleece to protect them from insects and pests.

THE FOUR CROP ROTATION GROUPS

A. *Potato Family*
This includes tomatoes, aubergines and peppers. Potatoes benefit from the addition of organic matter, and this in turn benefits the pea family the following year.

B. *Legumes*
This includes peas, broad beans, French and runner beans, sugar snap and mange-tout.

C. *Brassicas*
This includes broccoli, cabbages, calabrese, Brussels sprouts, Chinese cabbage, radishes and other oriental greens.

D. *Onions and Roots*
This includes all types of onions, chives, garlic, leeks and shallots, plus carrots, and parsnips. The onion family and root crops like soil that has been fertilized for a previous crop, so it makes sense that it follows on the site of last year's brassica family that will have been heavily fertilized with well-rotted manure. Root crops need no fresh manure and very little watering, and are grouped with onions in the rotation because they have similar requirements.

For the purposes of your notebook and when you are at the planning stages of what to grow, identify your divided plots as A, B, C and D.

NON-ROTATION CROPS

These are crops not related to the four main groups, which can be fitted in anywhere to fill gaps. They are undemanding, nutritionally speaking. They include chard, beetroot, and spinach, which benefit from manure that is high in nitrogen but are not dependent on it. Other non-rotation crops such as lettuces and salad leaves do not need high levels of nitrogen but will benefit from some organic matter to help lighten and enrich the soil. Crops such as rocket, parsley, chives, dill and coriander are not demanding of soil and can be sown in rows in any free space.

Marrows, courgettes and pumpkins thrive on moisture-retentive soil and the addition of well-rotted manure in the planting hole.

Sweetcorn is the least fussy about soil, so it too can be grown in any of the beds.

CATCH CROPS

This is the term for a crop that grows fast and fills a gap in the ground for a relatively short time. Plants such as beetroot, spinach, radish, coriander, rocket and lettuce make good catch crops because they germinate fast and mature quickly. They can also be picked young: as soon as the ground begins to fill up with slower developing crops, such as kale or broccoli.

Sow a catch crop of radish with a slow-to-mature crop such as parsnip or parsley. The radish will emerge quickly to mark out the row whilst the parsnip or parsley will come through later.

There is time to grow a crop of rocket between the supports of climbing beans which have been planted out in summer before the beans cast shade.

With sweetcorn, there is enough light to grow a row of dwarf French beans in the space between them.

Chapter 4

Clearing the Ground

This is strenuous work, so do it in stages, or organize a clearing and digging party with a fantastic picnic as reward. Many people actually enjoy digging, and if several people are involved a huge area of ground can be prepared fast.

You don't have to clear the whole plot in one go, but be aware that cleared ground won't remain weed-free for long. Make a realistic assessment of the time you have free, refer to your list of what you like to eat, and follow the first year rotation plan. For example, if it's early spring, prepare the bed for potatoes and get them planted; they will take care of themselves while you move on to the next area. Clear the bed for legumes and plant broad beans, or if it's late spring, fill it with runner and or French beans. Prepare a third rotation bed for onions and get them in. If it's late summer, refer to the calendar to see what to plant for winter and again link it to what you want to grow and your crop rotation plan.

Weeds

If you get into the habit of weeding regularly with a hoe and by hand, you will eventually weaken all weeds, including the strongest perennials.

If weed growth is more than 15 cm, use a scythe and/or shears and cut down adding to the compost bin (see pages 31–33 on *Compost*). To kill off the weed roots, you can now cover this area with a weed suppressant, ideally biodegradable like carpet or cardboard, or use a huge black polythene silage sheet that you can re-use over and over again. Whatever you use, be sure to secure it by digging the ends into the ground and holding down with stones or earth. Your neighbours won't thank you if your weed suppressors blow around the site.

If the ground has not been cultivated for more than a year it will be full of perennial weeds, and these may take six months to smother. If it was recently cultivated, the weeds will be young and should die within six weeks or so. Check after a month to see whether the weed roots are dead: there should be no sign of green. Uncover as much of the bed as you have time to prepare, fork the ground, lift out the dead roots, and rake the soil flat, ready for planting. Whilst you are working, the area under wraps is more or less looking after itself.

If you want to plant or sow in the ground immediately, and the weed growth lifts easily with a fork, then simply work your way over the plot forking and raking the weeds off the surface.

Couch grass can be a problem on uncultivated allotments. It looks like grass but has tougher leaves and a root up to 15 cm long. If you loosen the soil with a fork it is easily pulled out. It should be put in the refuse bin to take to the tip or burn later. You should check with your council first about any regulations concerning bonfires on allotments. Some allow small bonfires in the evening, but you can be fined if they get out of control.

Brambles

To get rid of brambles, wear thorn-proof gloves and either scythe the plants to ground level or cut them back with secateurs. Dig out the roots, as brambles dislike root disturbance so this will inhibit any re-growth. Put them in the refuse bin to take to the tip or burn later. Fork the ground over, removing any stones, and rake it flat.

Digging

Digging gets air into the soil, encouraging bacterial activity. It also exposes heavy soil to frost and snow, which will help to break it down. Use a fork or a spade to lift the soil, and turn it over, working in rows across the plot. Add organic matter on the surface after digging, raking it flat (see pages 30–37, *Improving the Soil*). If there is to be a gap of several months before the time is right to sow a crop, then use a green manure (see pages 34–35). This will stop valuable minerals being washed out, will inhibit fresh weed growth, and improve the texture and nutritional content of the soil.

Rotovating

If you have the entire plot to clear, you could hire a rotovator. This will break up the ground fast, but be warned: each weed root will be chopped into many pieces, and if it rains they may all re-grow. So after rotovating, when the soil will be looser, fork the ground over and remove the weeds from the surface with a rake.

Raised Beds

Raised beds are made up with imported topsoil and organic matter—think of them as giant grow-bags. If the allotment soil is very poor or waterlogged, it can take several years to improve it. Raised beds allow you to get on with growing crops immediately. Extra growing time is gained because the soil is higher and warms up earlier and no digging is involved.

To keep it simple, make four or eight raised beds and rotate them in the same way that you do for crops in the ground. The bed will be the width of the plot and deep enough to work comfortably from narrow paths on either side. The depth of the bed is the critical bit: you need to be able to weed and plant without stepping on the soil or straining your back. 1.2 metres is usual, but 1.5 metres is possible. Fork over the ground to loosen weeds and stones, and rake it flat. Mark out the shape with twine and skewers, and add topsoil until you have achieved a neat rounded surface across the entire bed. You may be able get topsoil from a builder; it's not uncommon to see a skip filled to the top with beautiful, rich soil. It is worth calling your local recycling depot, or community composting group if you have one, as they may have or know of a source. If you are making several raised beds, transporting soil may be a problem, so consider getting a delivery of organic topsoil delivered to the site. Or, less economically, buy 60 litre bags of organic planting medium from garden centres.

The height of raised beds varies but to start with, aim for 10 cm. Over the next four years you will gradually build it higher by adding well-rotted compost every autumn.

Paths run the length of the raised beds on either side; their size depends on how much space you have, but 38 cm wide is the minimum to get a decent foot space. You can define the raised beds with a frame made from pressure-treated planks or old floorboards. Cut them to size and use galvanized nails to secure them to corner pegs knocked into the ground. Garden centres and wood suppliers sell treated timber or, with the owners' permission, you can round up old floorboards from skips. Boards made from recycled bin bags and carriers are also available (see pages 154–155 for *Useful Addresses*). Raised beds in frames reduce the chance of soil spilling on to the path, and lessen exposure to wind and subsequent drying out.

Once the crop is over, remove the old roots, pull out any weeds and fork on a mulch of organic matter. This can be compost you have made or imported well-rotted farmyard manure. All planting, watering and weeding is done from the paths, so the soil remains in peak condition because it's never walked on. Keep the beds occupied with vegetables or use green manure.

Chapter 5

Soil Types

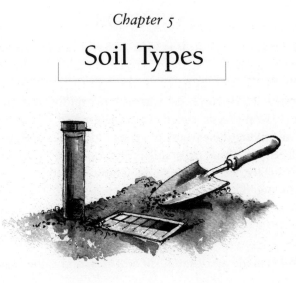

CLAY SOIL

You can recognize clay soil because it tends to hold water and is heavy; a spade will cut it into a neat cube that holds its shape. Clay soils are made up of clay or silt and are characterized by a fine texture that prevents drainage and can result in water-logged ground. This in turn can reduce air supply to plant roots, leaving them underdeveloped. The soil is also likely to get compacted in long dry summers, reducing root penetration and the level of oxygen necessary to sustain healthy growth. Clay can be slow to warm up in summer—not a huge disadvantage, but worth noting—and then after periods of sunshine can become bone hard.

You may think it's going to be an uphill struggle growing vegetables on clay soil, but in fact it has as many virtues as vices. First, once planted, the plants are well supported in this soil type: they stay where they are put and are less likely to flop over and get eaten by slugs. Also, most plants grow better in heavy soil because of the higher levels of nutrients retained by the tendency to waterlogging. So whilst it is difficult to sow seed directly into the ground with this soil type, small plants first raised in pots do very well (see pages 30–37, *Improving the Soil*).

SANDY SOIL

Sandy soil tends to dry out; it is light and will fall off the spade as you lift it from the ground. The main disadvantage of this soil is its coarse texture, which allows rain to drain through fast, taking moisture and nutrients with it. However, it warms up rapidly and is the perfect medium for sowing seeds directly into the ground. These will be quick to germinate, giving the earliest of crops in summer and, provided you regularly feed and water this soil type, you should get good results. Cover the surface with compost in winter to reduce nutrients from flooding out (see pages 30–37, *Improving the Soil*).

LOAMY SOIL

A loamy soil is made up of sand, silt and clay, and is the easiest to work with.

ACID SOIL

If the soil is too acid, bacteria (which are vital for breaking down the organic matter into humus) become less active. An indication of this is moss growing on the soil surface. Lime can be added to a very acid soil to make it neutral, but if your plants are doing well and there's evidence of worm activity, leave well alone. Adding large quantities of lime can upset the availability of other nutrients.

Brassicas, however, benefit from the addition of lime; it makes them less prone to clubroot. Spread 250 grams per square metre over the freshly dug surface in autumn or late winter. Leave it to be absorbed and do not add manure for at least one month.

ALKALINE SOIL

If the soil is too alkaline, the plants will be starved of essential trace elements as the nutrients get locked up in the chalky soil, and this will result in poor crops. If you find that your soil is very alkaline, then bucketloads of organic matter, especially pine needles, will help to redress the balance. Soil that is too alkaline for vegetable growing is rare, as the majority of soil in the British Isles tends to be slightly acid.

SOIL TEST

All soil types can be improved to give you the best results, but first you should buy a soil testing kit. Many people taking on an allotment never bother to analyse the soil. They assume the plot has been worked pretty thoroughly over the years, and a quick look at produce growing around them is a good indicator. However, a soil testing kit will give you the pH content, reflecting the amount of calcium—that is, chalk or lime—in the soil. The scale reads from 0 to 14, and a reading usually ranges between pH5 to pH8. The lower the figure, the stronger the soil acidity. Most plants grow best on a slightly acid soil, so about pH6 to 6.5 is ideal. The pH is simple to adjust by adding material that is acidic or alkaline as appropriate (see *Improving the Soil*).

Chapter 6

Improving the Soil

Early autumn and early spring are good times to start improving the ground. If your allotment has been recently cultivated, then wait until spring, when the earth is beginning to warm up and the texture of the soil is easier to work. If your allotment has not been worked recently, an autumn start is best to spread the workload. Avoid digging in the depths of winter, as the soil will stick to your boots and spade, taking out valuable nutrients.

You've identified your soil type, and now you may need to improve its structure. All soils are made up of humus and organic matter, and the level of both needs to be maintained for plants to grow properly. Nature's way of improving the soil is simple. Leaves (organic matter) fall on the ground; worms pull them through the surface, where micro-organisms aid their decomposition, turning them into rich humus. It is from this humus that the essential plant nutrients—phosphate, potash and nitrogen—are released. Phosphates are needed for healthy root formation, and potash affects the size and quality of fruit and flowers. Nitrogen is the most important nutrient of all and is responsible for improving leaves and stems. In effect you need to recreate nature's pattern by putting back into the ground large quantities of organic matter. This means you will need to dig in garden compost, farmyard manure, mushroom compost, leaf mould, seaweed or green manures. Generally there is no need to dig deeper than one spade depth—a 'spit deep', as it is called. However, enriching really poor soil and improving the drainage on heavy soils will require double digging two spits deep.

GARDEN COMPOST

Composting organic matter helps reduce the amount of rubbish in your dustbin, reduces methane on landfill sites and is a totally free soil improver. Once you start, you can become addicted to making compost and obsessed with saving every last scrap of organic matter imaginable for the compost bin. Keep an ice-cream container or the like under the sink for daily waste and when full, tip this into a bucket near the back door. When the bucket is full, take it to the compost bin.

You don't have to purchase a ready-made compost bin; you can simply pile the waste in a corner, and cover it with an old tarpaulin until it has decomposed. This is known as anaerobic composting, but it has some drawbacks. It will take longer to produce good compost because of a lack of oxygen, and since it doesn't get very hot, perennial weed seeds and bacteria will not be destroyed.

COMPOST BINS

Plastic conical bins with a lid are the easiest to use. You'll find them for sale in DIY stores or garden centres, but call your local authority first, as some councils supply them at reduced cost. Other models are available, but check they allow easy access to the rotted compost. Some have a tiny opening at the base that is too narrow to fit a spade in.

Slatted wood designs are simple to assemble, and the removable front makes it easy to dig out the compost. If you have time to make your own bins, aim for a pair side by side; this makes it easier to remove the top layer of uncomposted material into the adjacent bin so that you can get at the compost underneath. Each bin must be at least 90–120 cm high and the same width. Cover with a piece of tarpaulin, carpet, or heavy-duty plastic cut to size. It's important to place the containers on bare earth. Fork this over to encourage worms to get in and speed up the decomposing process. Keep the bins covered to keep the temperature up and to prevent rain from flooding valuable nutrients out.

It's difficult to predict how long it will take to form good compost, but with the right conditions you can achieve it within a few weeks; otherwise it can take between six to twelve months. Materials, weather, moisture content and warmth will all affect the speed of decomposition so be patient—eventually you will get results.

MAKING GOOD COMPOST

What to use
Waste from the garden such as lawn mowings, hedge clippings, spent vegetable plants, dead flowers, sawdust and wood ash, straw, hay and animal manures can all be composted. Twigs and other woody clippings are useful but should be used in moderation and chopped up before being mixed with softer materials. Compost heaps decompose faster if air is allowed to circulate, and small twigs encourage this by keeping the material separate. Quantities of woody material such as sweet corn stems and fruit canes are best shredded first.

Household waste such as vegetable peelings, tea leaves, coffee grounds, eggshells and more or less anything organic from the kitchen is all useful compost material. You should cut up the skins of citrus fruits to speed their decomposition.

You can add small quantities of corrugated paper or egg boxes shredded first. Bedding from hamster and guinea pig cages can also be added and is particularly useful if it includes some straw.

Once you get going, you'll be impatient to see results. Add nettles and comfrey leaves: these are known as activators because they break down fast and will speed things up. They are exceptionally high in potash, besides containing useful amounts of nitrogen and phosphorus.

A large quantity of brambles and woody prunings will take too long to break down, so should be excluded from the heap unless you can chop them up with a shredder. Set a small bundle aside to encourage wildlife if you have room, or burn and add the ash to the compost bin. Ash contains potash, an essential nutrient and particularly good for sandy soils that often lack potassium.

What not to use
Avoid adding annual weeds in flower, perennial weeds, especially couch grass, dandelions and thistles; instead put them in the refuse bin to burn

later. Do the same with any diseased or virus-infected plants. The heat generated by composting is rarely high enough to absolutely guarantee the destruction of unhealthy bacteria. NB: Don't use the content from cat litter trays—it's too gritty. And never put in waste proteins such as meat, fish or cheese, as these may attract rodents.

Layering

For efficient composting you need to vary the layers; ideally you need a third of a layer of nitrogen source (green waste such as grass and leaf) and two-thirds of a layer of carbon source (fibrous material such as stems, straw, peelings and roots).

If your compost looks dry, add water; if it looks too wet, add torn up newspaper that you have mixed with kitchen waste. Turning the heap every few weeks to add air helps to speed up decomposition, but this is time-consuming—if you vary the layers and include enough scrunched up cardboard and paper, your compost will just happen!

Two bins

The following method works well for cone composters or slatted bins. Fill your first bin up to the top and then start filling the second. When the second one is two-thirds full, the first will have sunk considerably. Lift the entire plastic cone off this first bin (or take the front off the slatted type). Fork the top layer (about half the contents) in to your second bin. This layer will be well on the way to decomposing, and underneath it you will find a substantial amount of good compost to spread on the beds. And you now have an empty bin to repeat the whole process again.

The compost is ready when it is dark brown and crumbly and smells sweetly of earth. Fork it into the surface of the beds to improve both the texture and nutrient content of the soil. However your homemade compost will not be suitable for sowing seeds or potting on seedlings. For this you'll need a bag of sterilized compost from garden centres.

MUSHROOM COMPOST

Spent mushroom compost consists mainly of straw composted with horse manure and ground chalk (lime), and is excellent for lightening heavy soil. The plant food value is low, as the mushrooms will have taken most of the nutrients, but when dug in, the lime will help to reduce acidity. You can buy it at garden centres, or look in the phone book or on the internet for a local mushroom farm.

FARMYARD MANURE

Horse and farmyard manure is rich in organic matter, and can often be obtained from riding stables and farms. Someone on site may be able to suggest a local supplier, and you can share a delivery with a neighbour. The best time to apply this and other soil improvers is at the end of autumn. As the ground opens up in icy weather, the organic matter will be drawn into the soil. Manure needs to be well rotted to go straight on the ground. If you buy it in spring and it seems to be quite fresh, then make a mound of it and cover with an old carpet to use a season later. It can be forked into the ground in spring or spread on the surface in autumn. The Soil Association recommends leaving farmyard manure from a non-organic farm for six months before using.

LEAF MOULD

This is another source of bulk to help break up heavy soil. You can make your own by bagging up fallen leaves in autumn, keep it for a year before spreading over the ground in winter. It is not high in nutrients but will improve the soil texture.

SOIL IMPROVER

Alternatively, order a peat-free soil improver from a garden centre or seed supplier (see *Useful Addresses*). This is usually a combination of super-concentrated manure and seaweed blend and comes in 60 litre bags for easy transporting to site.

SEAWEED

Seaweed is as rich in organic matter and nitrogen as farmyard manure. The alginate content encourages the break up of clay soils and binds sandy ones together. If you live near the coast you can gather some and either add it to your compost bin or dig it into the soil in autumn.

GREEN MANURES

Green manures are fast-growing crops that are sown in empty spaces to be dug back in to improve the fertility and texture of the soil. They cover the ground and suppress weeds and are more eco-friendly than black plastic.

SUMMER GREEN MANURES

Try **Mustard** *(Sinapsis alba)* and **Rape** *(Brassica napa var. napa)*. Both can be sown from spring through to autumn. They will be ready to dig back in between three and nine weeks from the date of sowing but catch them before they have formed flowers. They are at their most nutritious when young and succulent. If they are flowering, fork them out and add to the compost bin.

Essex red clover *(Trifolium pratense)* can be sown in summer or autumn. The sturdy stems will bulk up the humus, and are especially good for poor, sandy soil. The roots fix nitrogen from the atmosphere in the soil in the same way that peas and beans do, releasing it slowly for the crops that follow. Broadcast the seed (see pages 38–41, *Sowing and Planting*) any time from late winter through to early summer. Dig it back in just before it forms flowers. You can leave a few to flower since bees love clover, and they are useful pollinators for courgettes and marrows.

Buckwheat *(Fagopyrum esculentum)* is a summer-cropping green manure. The deep roots work their way down to the subsoil, drawing up nutrients to release into the topsoil when dug back in. The bulky stems improve the humus content. Broadcast seed any time from spring through to late summer, then dig in before the flowers have set and before winter. Leave a clump in flower to attract hoverflies, which in turn will feed on greenfly.

AUTUMN GREEN MANURES

In the autumn, when the last of the summer vegetables have been cleared away, sow winter manure crops to fill any vacant ground. This will help prevent rain from leaching out nutrients and reduce space for weeds to grow.

Winter crops to try are **Field Beans** *(Vicia faba)* and **Winter Tares** *(Vicia sativa)*, both of which have nitrogen-fixing nodules on the roots. These crops are only suitable for heavy soils, and should be sown in rows and dug back in the following spring. They will take a while to fully break down in the soil: you will see their decomposing stems and leaves for a good few months. This unrefined soil will be best suited to seedlings grown in biodegradable pots rather than broadcast seed.

LIQUID MANURE

This is not a soil improver, in the sense that it does not change the texture of the earth. But it will improve the nutritional content of the soil and it is easy to make your own.

Comfrey, with its blue flowers and hairy leaves, makes inexpensive liquid manure and is often found growing on or about allotment sites. It's worth buying if you haven't got it: the plant to look for is the **Russian comfrey Symphytum 'Bocking 14'**. You'll need about ten plants, planting them 60 cm apart, close to your compost bins. Cut them back to base in spring, when the plant is about 45 cm high. It will re-grow again in six weeks, and you can repeat the operation.

Cut up the cropped leaves and put them in the bottom of a barrel or similar size refuse bin—you will need to drill a hole in the base near the edge. This container should be supported on bricks, high enough to place a jam jar under the hole. The comfrey leaves will need to be weighed down with a piece of wood or a brick. As the leaves decompose, the liquid manure drips into the jar. You then dilute it ten to fifteen times with water and use it as a general fertilizer to water any of your plants. If that sounds like too much effort, you can just cut up the leaves and add to the compost bin.

Nettles make a nutritious feed using the same method as comfrey. They are less attractive plants, with a nasty sting, so you might not want to maintain a bed of them! But if you are clearing a large area of nettles, you could make liquid manure as a one-off. Thereafter any nettles that appear should be rooted out, chopped up with a spade and put in the compost bin.

CONCENTRATED ORGANIC FERTILIZERS

If you follow the principles of soil improving combined with crop rotation, you will get healthy crops. However nitrogen, phosphates and potash are rapidly taken out of the soil by greedy plants. Spreading well-rotted compost on the surface of the beds is the cheapest and most organic way of enriching your soil. If you have no compost, an occasional feed of commercial organic fertilizer, specifically balanced for vegetable growing, can be added before sowing at fortnightly intervals throughout the growing season. It is available in pellet form to scatter over the soil surface, or in powder form to mix in a watering can. Blood fish and bone is the most common mixture, and contains all the essential elements. Ash, hood and horn is also available as good supplementary feed.

Sowing and Planting

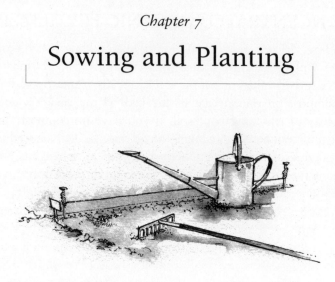

Always fill any prepared ground to the maximum to reduce space for weeds. Most produce will sit in the soil without spoiling until you are ready to crop it.

MAKING A SEED BED

To make a seed bed, prepare the ground by forking it over and pulling out any weeds. The soil needs to be firm, free of stones and lumps of soil, and raked till the soil crumbs resemble breadcrumbs. Some seedlings hate to be re-planted, so should be sown directly in the ground and thinned out as they come through. Others can be lifted and planted in straight rows when they are big enough to handle. You can also sow into seed trays or pots to transplant the seedlings later.

SOWING IN THE GROUND

Preparing to sow

Early spring is the best time to start, as soon as you can trust that there will be no late frost. When the surface of the soil has a dry thin top layer and a moist section immediately below, the ground is ready to be forked and raked. Another test is to walk on the surface; if the soil clings to your boots, the ground is still too wet and you will need to wait another week or so.

Break down the lumpy soil by bashing with the side of the fork and prod into the ground to about 5–8 cm (no deeper), twisting the fork to loosen the soil. The layer below 5–8 cm will contain nutrients either from last year's mulch or from decaying leaves dropped in autumn. This layer will feed the new plants, so should not be disturbed. Rake across the forked ground to obtain a fine tilth.

Sowing

You may not sow all your seeds in one go, but the prepared ground can be left ready for subsequent sowing over the next few weeks. Mark a row across the plot with twine tied to two skewers, stand back to make sure it is correctly aligned, and adjust the string accordingly. Make a channel with your trowel or the handle of the rake to the depth suggested on the seed packet—anything between 1–5 cm. Water the base of the seed drill before you sow, using the watering can with a fine rose head. Pour seeds into one hand and with the other pinch a few and drop them along the row. If you do this fast you will get a better spaced sowing. Pull the soil back over the seeds with the flat side of the rake. Leave the twine *in situ* until the seedlings appear. Some vegetables take several weeks to germinate. Always mark the row with a label (the seed packet pierced with a bamboo cane is fine as a temporary solution, but will soon disintegrate in wind and rain).

You can assist germination by covering the seeds with a cloche, polytunnel or fleece to advance crops by at least two weeks (see pages 47–51, *Cultivation*). Cover only half the row at a time and you will spread the harvesting time.

Seed tape is available for some vegetables. The seed is held between two paper strips appropriately spaced, and you simply lay the tape down in the prepared channel and cover with soil.

Some seeds are made into tiny balls with protective coating to make them easy to handle. This makes spacing easy and avoids thinning out. These will need to be sown in a well-soaked drill and kept watered to encourage germination.

Broadcast seed

Prepare the ground and scatter the seeds evenly before dragging the rake over the surface to lightly cover the seeds with soil. This method of sowing is used for crops that require little thinning such as beetroot or radishes, and plants that hate to be disturbed such as carrots and parsnips.

When sowing early in the season, wait until the first seeds have germinated before sowing again, because later sowings grow more quickly (it gets warmer) and may result in simultaneous cropping.

SOWING IN SEED TRAYS

This will allow you to start plants off at home either on a sunny windowsill or in a cold frame. Most seeds germinate at around 18°C/65°F indoors in early spring, or in a cold frame outside a month later.

Plastic seed trays and flowerpots are re-useable each season and can be cleaned easily. Experiment with containers supplied with supermarket products, but be sure to pierce the base for drainage.

For sowing seeds, use a commercial seed compost—there are a number of organic composts available. Fill the tray level to the top with new compost that is slightly moist and firm it down with your hand. Pinch the seeds between your thumb and finger rather than pouring out of the packet. Large seeds should be placed individually. Cover with a thin layer of compost and label the tray with the name of the seed and date sown.

POTTING ON

Most seeds germinate within a week, and the earlier they are thinned and potted on to a single 9 cm pot the better. When two leaves are clearly visible, gently hold one of them whilst lifting the seedling out of the compost. Use a plastic label or spoon handle to gently ease it out and make a hole in the new pot of compost to drop the seedling in. Firm the soil around the plant and water with a fine rose spray. This is fiddly, but less damage is done to the roots if they are potted on this early.

HARDENING OFF

Your seedlings need steady growth in the warm before 'hardening off' outside. Hardening off is the term used for gradually toughening up young plants prior to planting in the ground. The standard method is to leave them in an open cold frame or protected situation outdoors for longer periods each day. After a few weeks they can stay out at night in a closed cold frame or covered with fleece. This gradually prepares them for life in the ground.

SOWING IN MODULES

Invest in a pot maker—these are available in garden centres and mail order catalogues. All you need is newspaper to form the pot, which can then be planted with the seedling in the ground. Some vegetables hate being pricked out or transplanted; these young plants will have their own root ball and suffer the minimum disturbance as you ease them, pot and all, into the ground. You can purchase ready-made biodegradable pots, but they add considerably to the cost of your organic vegetables since they cannot be re-used. Choose a variety of sizes: the largest for tomatoes, courgettes, beans etc, and the smaller for brassicas, lettuce, carrots and onions.

Pre-formed multi-celled plastic plug trays are a good investment and can be washed and re-used for years. They usefully aid the propagation of up to 140 seedlings in one go. This is ideal for leeks, as you may need this many to fill a bed. Tap the compost into the shallow cells and sow one seed in each. Carefully label each section if you are sowing a variety of different seeds. When the plant has four leaves, tilt the tray and push the plug of earth from underneath to ease the seedling out. Depending on the vegetable you can either pot on to a bigger pot or plant the plug directly in the prepared ground.

PLANTING

To save time and for some inspiring, instant results, buy some trays of young vegetable plants from the garden centre rather than growing everything from seed. Follow the instructions for planting depth and spacing, water carefully at soil level, and firm in.

FILLING GAPS

Some frost-tender plants such as beans, courgettes, pumpkin, sweetcorn and tomatoes can't be put out until early summer, so use a catch crop in the preceding weeks (see pages 20–22, *Crop Rotation*).

Chapter 8

Protecting your Plants

You can extend the growing season in both spring and autumn by using various forms of crop protection. Look in skips for discarded glazed windows that you can use to make inexpensive cold frames, and reuse large plastic water bottles to make cloches. Manufactured frames and cloches are available made with lightweight plastics and synthetic fibres, keeping the costs down and allowing you to experiment. You will be able to re-use these products every season.

CLOCHES

You can assist germination by covering newly sown seeds with a cloche. When the seeds are sturdy enough to be planted on, you can simply lift the cloche and place it on another patch of newly sown seeds.

You can make individual cloches from large plastic water bottles. Cut the bottom off and unscrew the top so that air can circulate. Manufactured cloches come in a variety of shapes and sizes. They allow you to sow in advance of the weather, both warming the soil before planting and protecting young plants from early or late frosts.

HORTICULTURAL FLEECE

Fleece is a versatile alternative to a fixed structure, but will need to be secured with small bags filled with soil or stones or purpose-made pegs. Use it to cover beds a few weeks before sowing to warm the ground. Allow the young seedlings to grow for a week or two before covering again with the fleece, pleating extra fleece material along the edges. You can leave it on until the crop is ready for harvesting, releasing the pleating as the plants get taller. It will allow light, air and water in, whilst protecting plants from flying pests.

MESH OR NETTING

This is available in garden centres and is sold by the metre. It is used for supporting vegetables and protecting against bird damage. It can be secured over a seedbed to inhibit slugs.

POLYTUNNELS

These offer the same protection as cloches but cover a wider area. The simplest models are made of polythene stretched over wire hoops on legs that are pushed in the ground. The range is huge, but aim for ones that are easy to move around the site, secure in the ground and tough enough to survive windy weather.

COLD FRAMES

A cold frame is invaluable for hardening off seedlings raised in the warm. It offers a halfway house between indoors and outdoors, and is basically a box with a lift-off glazed roof. You can buy modern lightweight models or make one yourself.

Stack up old bricks on either side to a height of 30 cm and place an old glazed window frame on top. Build it on bare earth next to the shed for added protection. You can also use wooden boards to support the window: cut them slightly shorter than the window frame and nail together at the four corners.

Chapter 9

Design

Part of the charm of the allotment is the way individual plot holders appropriate the space provided. Some build compost bins out of rusty corrugated metal; others create bird scarers from cut up strips of coloured polythene or old CDs. There is usually a motley assortment of receptacles on site to collect rainwater or material for a bonfire. This pragmatic approach is refreshing and takes the pressure off striving for a perfect plot, especially in the first few years.

That said, bountiful beds are what you are after. You will be proud to have achieved them and motivated by their beauty to maintain them.

THINK BIG

At the planning stage, and with the principles of crop rotation in mind, make sure you aim for large blocks of crops. Don't worry about excess; there are few vegetables that grow so quickly that they produce faster than you can harvest them. At worst you may find yourself eating lettuce most days in the summer.

There are many interesting recipes to vary the preparation of any one crop, and if you get bored with a vegetable, freeze it, cooked if necessary, or give it away and recruit someone to organic vegetable growing! Presenting a friend with a basket of freshly cut spinach, lettuce, herbs and beans has to be one of the greatest pleasures of growing your own. It's far more frustrating to have finished picking the one row you have of something delicious and then be forced to face a year's wait for more.

In garden design, successful borders can be achieved by placing tall spiky plants next to fat round ones to break up the horizontal plane and to achieve a tension. The same will work on an allotment. Onions, leeks and chives will give vertical interest and combine well with the rounded form of lettuces and cabbages, even when seen from their different beds.

Moss curled parsley has an interesting texture and can be used to define the edge of any bed. The same goes for flat leaf parsley and chives.

WINTER BEDS

Aim to completely fill the beds with winter vegetables. They mostly look after themselves and will keep you in organic produce at the quietest time of year.

Squash and pumpkins fruit in early autumn, and offer some dramatic colours and strange forms at the quieter end of the growing season. Their huge ivory-white or steel-blue balls will sit comfortably on the soil until the first frosts. Smaller varieties, some of which are orange and pear-shaped, others the size of tennis balls with creamy striped skins, will liven up the ground for weeks as well as providing late season produce.

The blue-green strap-like leaves of leeks look beautiful lit by winter sunshine. And the sight of fat, purple-sprouting broccoli emerging from silver-grey, veined leaves, makes a trip to the allotment in the cold really worthwhile. **Cavola Nero di Toscano**, a curly–leafed kale, will keep growing through winter, the blistered dark green leaves adding drama until the spring.

SUMMER BEDS

Be adventurous—there are many unusual and brightly coloured vegetables to choose from. The green, red, yellow and white leaves of rainbow chard look stunning planted next to a row of purple dwarf beans.

The leaves of courgettes make a bold statement from early summer until the end of autumn: their leaves dark green, splashed with silver or bold yellow brush strokes. Try the round courgette **Leprechaun** for a change, or the butter-yellow, glossy skinned variety **Taxi**.

Lettuces offer a great opportunity to add colour and texture to the entire plot. To grow two rows of lettuce across the bed you need empty ground measuring a minimum of 50 cm wide. This can then be divided into three blocks. Sow two rows of a red-leafed variety such as **Bijou**, but only in the first third of the ground. Follow this with a block of **Frisby**, which is green, and in the third block try **Lolla Rossa** which has a frilly leaf and repeats the red.

Whilst the aim of growing produce is led by practicalities, bear the following points in mind:

- Grow large blocks of each vegetable for visual impact.
- Contrast texture, colour and form where possible.
- Plant large quantities of winter crops to fill the space in an otherwise quiet season.

Chapter 10

Cultivation

HOEING

You have to keep the upper hand with weeds, and there may be times when you feel you are losing it. After a warm wet spell they can emerge as fast as your newly sown seeds, smothering their development and competing for nutrients. Regular hoeing is essential, and should be done the moment weed seedlings are seen, when they are young enough to be hoed out of the ground and left to die. Never hoe deeply: the object is to sever the weed from its roots using a push-pull action.

An onion hoe is useful for hoeing between closely grown plants as the shorter shaft makes it easier to control. You use this by walking backwards, drawing the hoe over the surface towards you.

Only hoe in dry weather, when the weeds will be at their weakest. Keep the blade sharp on the hoe with a cutting stone; hoes are useless when blunt.

MULCHING

Mulching the surface around plants helps keep weeds down and conserves water, generally improving the condition of the soil. Prepare the ground well by removing all weeds, and incorporate compost and organic fertilizers into the soil before mulching. A mulch is traditionally made from compost, well-rotted farmyard manure, seaweed or straw. The following also make good organic mulches:

Newspaper

Use double thickness, overlapping the two sheets by 5 cm. Hold the paper in place with dampened soil sprinkled round the edge and on the overlap to stop the paper blowing away. Plant seedling plants through it, or use to warm up the ground for a few weeks whilst you are waiting to sow. The *Financial Times* is not recommended because of the pink dye.

Bracken

If bracken is available in large quantities, use the fronds to make a thick mulch. These release potash, which is particularly beneficial around the base of gooseberries.

Cardboard

Flattened boxes will suppress weeds for one season before they biodegrade. They can be held down with planks or bricks.

Shredded prunings

If you have access to a shredder, use it to shred your woody prunings into a mulch. Leave the chipped material in a corner for a few months and add grass mowings and nettles to the heap to improve the nitrogen levels.

Woodchip

This can absorb valuable nitrogen from the soil so should be mixed with an organic nitrogen fertilizer before spreading over the beds.

Ornamental bark

This is recycled compost from conifer bark. Unlike woodchip, it will not deplete the soil of nitrogen and will improve the condition of the soil.

Check with your local authority: some now shred green waste to sell back as mulch. Wherever possible, get into the habit of using these organic mulches.

Straw

A thick straw mulch is traditionally used to grow strawberries and squash, the aim being to conserve water whilst keeping the fruit off the damp soil. The straw will biodegrade eventually, and a new supply can be brought in.

MAN-MADE MULCHES

Geotextiles

There are many fabrics sold by the metre, some biodegradable and some not, which can be used as mulches. Whilst they are not as environmentally friendly as organic methods, they do cut down time spent weeding and watering, and will last on average for 15 years.

These man-made fabrics are water- and air-permeable, and either woven or spun. Potatoes, strawberries and squashes can be planted through them. Prepare the ground with plenty of well-rotted farm or garden compost and cover with the sheeting, securing it down with stones or digging it in to trenches back-filled with soil. In spring, this covered area will warm up early and should be entirely weed-free.

Sow seed potatoes by rolling back the fabric, planting the tubers and then covering again. As the leaves emerge, bumps will be seen at regular intervals under the sheet. Carefully cut a cross-shaped slit and ease the leaves through. Some sheeting is marked with a grid to make spacing and planting simpler. You follow the grid size to space your plants in the ground.

Strawberries can be grown in the same way, and if you have a large bed this will reduce time spent weeding. The squash family does well growing through water permeable sheeting. The aim is for the water to run off the surface, leaving the squash basking on a sun-baked dry surface. You will need to plant through the sheeting material, not under it. Prepare the ground in the usual way, adding lots of well-rotted manure, secure the sheeting over the bed, and cut a cross-shaped slit with the appropriate spacing between each plant. Dig through the slit with a trowel and add some rich farmyard manure into the planting hole as they are very greedy feeders. Firm the plant in and water well before securing the material firmly around the plant stem. Regular watering will still be necessary throughout the growing time. Direct the water through the gap where the plant comes through.

Black sheet polypropylene

This is a non-permeable material, sometimes known as 'silage sheet'. It is sold by the metre at garden centres, but as a non-renewable resource it is expensive both environmentally and materially. It can be used to cover newly prepared ground to warm the soil prior to planting, or to cover a weed-ridden area whilst you are preparing ground elsewhere.

Polypropylene landscape fabric
This is water-permeable and plants can grow through it—rain will reach the roots and moisture is conserved. It is long lasting and can be used for several years.

Biodegradable fleece
This is sold by the metre and is usually 1.5 metres wide. It can be used around plants to protect from frost or planted through. It is expensive and will need to be replaced every one or two seasons.

WATER

If the leaves on various plants are dull and followed by wilting, this is almost certainly due to too little water. Growth will be checked, plants run to seed and young fruit may drop off. If you don't live on-site, you may have to make a daily trip to the allotment to water in really hot weather. If possible, water in the evening, as the ground will remain wet for longer and moisture will have a chance to reach the roots. Avoid watering in strong sunlight as you may scorch wet leaves.

Invest in a water butt or two, or other receptacles to store rainwater.

SUPPORTS FOR CLIMBING PLANTS

Use recycled poles and sticks where possible. If you have a garden, then save the prunings from woody shrubs for pea sticks. Woods are full of fallen branches from young trees, and these make excellent bean poles. Look in the phone book for suppliers: fencing contractors often coppice hazel and chestnut fences themselves and may have offcuts to give away.

Canes

Canes are a simple solution and can be stored in the shed to reuse each year. Runner beans and climbing French beans will need 3 metre high canes.

To make a row for climbing beans, space the canes three footprints apart with the same spacing between the two rows, and tie the tops together to secure them. Stabilize by tying a horizontal cane the length of the row tied in where the upright canes meet (see illustration opposite). The beans will twine and can be tied with string if necessary.

Wigwam

A wigwam takes up less room and is assembled by pushing three or four canes into the ground, tying them at the top.

Post and wire

An alternative support is to drive a strong post deep into the ground at each end of a row and run a wire across. This is most useful for a permanent crop such as raspberries and blackberries. The posts will need to be about 3 metres tall and wires spaced across at 20 cm intervals. Tie the plants in as they grow.

Twigs

Twigs cut from brushwood make a good support for shorter climbing plants such as peas and mange tout. They will need to be at least 1.5 metres tall, with several branches to take the weight of the produce. Alternatively, purchase pea sticks from the garden centre. You can drape the support with mesh or netting for the peas to clamber through.

Chapter 11

Harvesting and Storing

HARVESTING

Ideally you will be cropping your produce as soon as it is at the peak of tenderness and flavour. Even three days after picking, your produce will still be fresher than anything you might find at the supermarket. Many crops can be left in the ground for several weeks until you need them.

Take care when harvesting your crops:

- Avoid pulling peas and beans down the stem, as an open wound may encourage virus infection. Just pinch or cut the pods off.
- Cut cabbages, broccoli, pumpkins and courgettes from the main plant with a sharp knife, taking care not to dislodge the plant roots in the ground.
- Gently push a spade in wide of the foliage on root crops such as potatoes, carrots, parsnips and artichokes, to avoid splitting the skin with the tool.
- All cut-and-come-again plants such as salad leaves and lettuces should be cut from the main plant with scissors or pinched between finger and thumb.

STORING

There will be times in the summer season when you will have a glut, and there are several things you can do:

Broad beans, French beans and peas. Frozen vegetables are never as good as fresh ones, but peas and beans are definitely worth freezing. Simply pod and freeze them in bags.

Borlotti and haricot beans. These are best dried and stored. Leave them on the plant until the skins look leathery, then dry on newspaper before podding and storing in jars. You will need to soak these dried beans before cooking, as you do with bought ones.

Gooseberries, raspberries, and red- and blackcurrants. These all freeze well or can be made into purées or jam.

Potatoes. These will need to be kept in the dark in dry sacks tied at the top. Do not use polythene bags, and only store main or late crops.

Carrots, parsnips, beetroot and celeriac. These will keep well in dry airy spaces packed in wooden crates between sand or sawdust. Make sure the flesh is undamaged when you store them.

Onions and garlic. These should be dried in the sun after cropping, then tied into strings. Alternatively hang them in nets in a dry larder.

If space is a problem for storing, then make soups and purées from any excess vegetables and freeze these in their cooked form.

SAVING SEED

This can become wonderfully addictive, and is relatively easy and economical. Almost any vegetable or herb that is allowed to go to flower will produce a viable seed head as long as it is allowed to ripen fully on the plant. It is ripe when the seed head has gone from green to brown. Collect the seeds in envelopes, carefully identified, and keep them in a dry warm place till the following year.

The easiest plant to experiment with is the seed of cut-and-come-again salad leaves. These often suddenly go to flower in warm weather. The flower left to ripen will generate a good amount of seed that can be sown back in there and then, or saved as above.

Leave a pod or two on peas or runner beans until they are brown, and dry then store in a paper bag till next summer. If rain threatens, pick them and leave in the airing cupboard for a few weeks. Shallots and garlic produce clusters of bulbs that can be separated, dried and kept till the next planting season.

Most bought seeds will remain viable for several years but must be kept in a cool dry place. Parsnip seeds are the exception, as they have a very short life span and will need to be bought fresh every year.

Chapter 13

Gardener's Calendar

JANUARY

Sow
Early radishes and lettuces in a cold frame.

Crop
Cabbages, kale, leeks and parsnips.

Also . . .
Look at seed catalogues and start planning your beds. Order seeds for the spring sowing.

Purchase and 'chit' seed potatoes.

Net currant bushes to prevent birds eating the new buds.

FEBRUARY

Sow
Early beetroot, broad beans, spinach, summer cabbage, calabrese, globe artichoke and lettuce indoors from seed in trays or pots.

Early beetroot, carrots, lettuce, spring onions, salad leaves, spinach outside from seed under cloches in warmer areas.

Onion sets, shallots and garlic outside, as soon as the ground is workable.

Plant rhubarb and cover with a pot to force early stalks.

Plant tubers of Jerusalem artichokes from now until April.

Crop
Early sprouting broccoli, leeks, cabbages, kale, parsnips and celery.

Also . . .
Apply a general fertilizer to the ground before sowing early crops.

Apply organic fertilizer to over-wintered crops such as broad beans, onions, and spring cabbages when growth begins.

Apply organic fertilizer to gooseberries and currants.

Cut back newly planted cane and bush fruits.

Cut down autumn-fruiting raspberry canes to ground level and mulch.

Dig if the ground is dry.

Add lime to the areas that need it, such as the brassica bed.

Continue to chit potatoes.

MARCH

Sow
Towards the end of the month, transplant seedlings sown in trays indoors in February singly into 9 cm pots, keep in the cold frame till the end of the month, then plant in the ground.

Sow leeks in a seed tray to thin later to two each in 9 cm pots. These can be kept in the cold frame until the end of March, then planted in the ground.

Sow celery in trays on a warm windowsill and keep moist.

Peas, and broad beans in pots.

Early beetroot, lettuce, salad leaves, carrots, radishes, spring onions, leaf beet seeds directly in the ground.

Plant onion sets, garlic and shallots if you didn't get them in last month.

Plant early potatoes as soon as the ground is dry enough.

Continue to plant tubers of Jerusalem artichokes.

Crop

Sprouting broccoli, cabbages, kale, leeks and parsnips.

Also . . .

Mulch with organic matter all soft fruits.

Lift mint every two years and divide.

Hoe weeds regularly before they get too large.

Be vigilant for slugs.

APRIL

Sow

Kale, broad beans, kohlrabi, leeks and parsnip seeds directly into the ground.

Beans, courgettes, squash, pumpkins and sweet corn at end of month behind glass, to plant out at the end of May.

Purchase seedling vegetables from garden centre and plant out.

Plant onion sets, shallots and garlic if not done already.

Plant all hardy vegetables started indoors in March in the ground at end of this month.

Hardy annual flowers directly in ground.

Repeat sow salad leaves, lettuce, rocket, parsley, coriander, carrots and spring onions directly in ground.

Finish planting 'chitted' potatoes.

Plant one-year-old crowns of asparagus.

Crop

Broccoli, autumn lettuces, cabbages, kale and leeks should now be ready for a final picking.

Also . . .

Keep ahead of the slugs—they love young seedlings.

Clear beds of winter vegetables and prepare ground.

Cover summer brassicas and carrots with mesh to keep flying insects off.

Give a liquid feed to autumn-sown garlic.

MAY

Sow

Brussels sprouts, broccoli, winter cabbage and kale in seedbeds.

Continue to sow peas, lettuce, salad leaves, spring onions, beetroot, rocket, carrots, coriander and kohlrabi directly in the ground.

A row of marigolds at the base of sweet peas and nasturtiums near the broad beans to protect against blackfly.

Harden off celery plants to set outdoors at the end of the month.

Cut flowers.

Plant beans, squash, courgettes, sweet corn and pumpkins in the ground at the end of this month.

Crop

Not a great month for cropping but you may have some cabbages and spinach left from winter.

Lettuces, salad leaves, rocket and spring onions should be big enough to pick now.

Also . . .

Thin rows of seedlings, including annual flowers which do much better when they have space around them.

Prepare ground for leeks.

Stake broad beans.

Put straw under and around strawberries to keep soil off the fruit.

Continue to weed, hoe and mulch.

JUNE

Sow

Continue to sow French beans, runner beans, peas, beetroot, carrots, kohlrabi, spinach beet, lettuces and salad leaves directly in the soil

Plant out seedlings of leeks, cabbages, celeriac, courgettes, squash, pumpkins, outdoor tomatoes, calabrese and purple sprouting broccoli.

Crop

Pick soft fruit.

Winter-sown broad beans, peas, early potatoes, garlic and shallots.

Salad leaves, rocket and cut and come again lettuces should be picked regularly.

Also . . .

Dry shallots and garlic in the sun.

Water crops in dry weather and mulch to conserve moisture and to keep down the weeds.

Stake tomatoes, peas and dwarf beans.

Tie raspberry canes to wires.

Net soft fruit against birds.

JULY

Sow

Kale, spinach beet, Chinese greens, cabbages, winter lettuces and radishes directly in the ground.

Crop

This month you should get bumper crops of strawberries, raspberries, red- and blackcurrants, and rhubarb.

French and runner beans.

Tomatoes, courgettes and potatoes, cabbages, spinach, beetroot and lettuces will be at their best.

Also . . .

Hoe and water regularly.

Earth up main crop potatoes.

Cut down raspberry canes as soon as the fruit is over and start to tie in this year's canes.

AUGUST

Sow

Look ahead and sow cabbages, perpetual spinach, radicchio, winter lettuces and spring onions in a seed bed or in pots to transplant later.

Parsley for winter cropping.

Crop

Sweet corn, onions, French beans, runner beans, peas, calabrese, cabbages, carrots, courgettes and potatoes.

All remaining soft fruit.

Also . . .

Weed thoroughly, water and mulch.

Stake all tall plants to keep them off the ground.

Pinch out the top of outdoor tomatoes when 4–5 trusses have set. As the days shorten, remove the canes from tomatoes and lay the plants on straw to continue ripening.

Dry onions on the surface of the bed if sunny, or indoors in the dry before stringing up.

Continue to prepare new strawberry beds and plant out runners.

SEPTEMBER

Sow

Swiss chard, perpetual spinach and mixed winter salad leaves directly in the ground. Lamb's lettuce can be grown under cloches for winter salads.

Plant out seedling spring cabbages, perpetual spinach, chicory and radicchio.

Crop

Crop French beans, runner beans, broad beans, lettuces, courgettes, marrow, carrots, sweet corn, cabbages, peas, main crop potatoes and autumn raspberries.

Also . . .

Draw soil around celeriac and leeks.

Cut off this summer's fruiting blackberry and raspberry canes at ground level and tie in the new canes.

Order new fruit bushes for winter planting.

OCTOBER

Sow

Broad beans and peas directly in the ground to overwinter.

Garlic and onion sets.

Continue planting seedling spring cabbage and spring greens until mid-month.

Crop

Lift and store carrots, beetroot, winter radishes.

Leave cabbages, kale, celeriac, Jerusalem artichokes and parsnips in the ground until you need them. Sprouts may be ready but are best left until after the first frost.

Pick haricot, flageolet and borlotti beans, leaving them to dry in a basket in a cool shed before podding them to store.

Continue harvesting globe artichokes, beetroot and kohlrabi.

Lift all main crop potatoes for storing in paper sacks in a dry, dark cupboard.

Also . . .

Clear beds of crops that are over and fork the ground, clearing any weeds as you go.

Buy farm manure, soil improver or mushroom compost to fork into the empty beds.

Sow a winter green manure if bed is to remain empty till spring.

Earth up leeks and celery.

Lift mature clumps of rhubarb and pull apart to fist-size pieces. Plant these 1 metre apart in well-manured soil.

NOVEMBER

Sow

Peas and broad beans can still be sown in reasonable weather.

New soft fruit bushes and rhubarb can be planted if the ground is workable.

Autumn and Japanese onion sets and garlic if you haven't already.

Crop

Celery, leeks, sprouts, parsnips, Jerusalem artichokes and cabbages can still be cropped.

Swiss chard leaves may be a bit leathery but the rib can still be cooked.

Also . . .

Digging is best done this month before the weather gets cold and wet. Dig in well-rotted farmyard manure or compost where the peas and beans, onions and leeks, celery and spinach are to grow next year.

Cut globe artichoke stems to the ground and draw soil over to protect them.

Lift mint roots and divide up before planting in a pot to use over winter. Keep in a conservatory or on sunny windowsill.

DECEMBER

Sow

Plant onion sets if you haven't yet done so.

Crop

Celery, leeks, parsnips, sprouts, cabbages, Jerusalem artichokes and spinach beet.

Also . . .

Get out your notebook and remind yourself of successes and failures, what you have cropped in the last three months and what is still to come. The notes are to remind you at the sowing and planting stages and are particularly useful when planning autumn and winter crops.

Protect bay, rosemary and marjoram in severe weather either with a cloche or fleece.

Share a delivery of well-rotted farmyard manure with others on the allotment.

Part Two
A-Z OF VEGETABLES, FRUIT, HERBS AND FLOWERS

Introduction

SEEDS OR PLANTS?

Seeds are one of nature's miracles: within a season or two, an inexpensive seed packet will have magically turned into dozens of nourishing plants. And growing from seed is by far the cheapest way to stock your allotment. But unless you have a greenhouse it may be impractical to grow everything from seed, and there's a limit to the number of sunny windowsills available early in the season. Some local authorities allow small greenhouses, but all forbid using a concrete base. This limits the stability and size, and if your allotment is on a slope, rules it out as an option. So buy some seedling plants as well; they give a huge boost to the confidence, and although not as cost-effective as seed packets, they still work out at only a tenth of the price of buying vegetables in a shop.

WHERE TO BUY

The seed suppliers listed at the back of the book are included because they have a fantastically wide range of interesting produce. Many have reintroduced old favourites; others are offering new aphid-resistant varieties; and, increasingly, organic seeds are available. Some seed catalogues are now offering starter plants by post, and garden centres carry a huge range of vegetable seedling plants as well as seeds. Other useful sources are farmers' markets, WI stalls and car boot sales.

VARIETIES

I have recommended two varieties, chosen for their exceptional flavour and because many of them are available as organic seeds. There are many more, so have fun and experiment with different varieties.

PESTS AND DISEASES

The most common pests and diseases are mentioned after each entry. Refer to *Troubleshooting* (pages 148–153) for advice on controlling them.

RECIPES

I have included some very simple recipes, chosen because they are an interesting way to bring out the flavour of the produce. They are for 4 people.

Vegetables

ASPARAGUS
Asparagus officinalis

Asparagus has a reputation for being difficult to grow, taking years to establish and requiring lots of space. In fact, if you purchase one-year-old crowns you should get a small crop in the first year after planting.

When to Plant
Mid-spring.

Where to Plant
Asparagus is a permanent crop that requires a bed outside the rotation plan, with free-draining soil that has been enriched with well-rotted manure. Plant the crowns in rows 45 cm apart, with 1.50 metres between rows. Alternatively plant randomly but keep to this spacing. Plant a minimum of ten plants to make a decent crop.

Cultivation
Keep the bed weed-free. Cut back to ground level in late autumn and mulch with compost or well-rotted manure in winter. If a frost threatens in late spring, cover the emerging shoots with fleece. In the second year after planting and thereafter you can draw the earth up the stems to a height of 10 cm to increase the white stem.

Harvesting & Storing
Cut the spears when they are about 18 cm long, inserting a knife in 6 cm below the soil level. You will get a full crop from the fourth year, when each plant should produce 20–30 spears over a three-month period.

Varieties

Purple Passion is a dark purple, very tender asparagus and will crop the second year after planting.

Jersey Giant was bred at the Jersey Asparagus Centre and is thick and succulent.

Pests & Diseases

Slugs, asparagus beetle, violet root rot.

Asparagus Vinaigrette

It's a challenge to enhance the subtle flavour of asparagus, but the lemon in this dressing gives a delicious kick. Bring a pan of salted water to the boil, add 24 washed asparagus spears and cook till tender, about 5–6 minutes depending on thickness. Drain and dress immediately with 4 tbsps of virgin olive oil mixed with 1 tbsp of lemon juice, sea salt and black pepper.

AUBERGINES
Solanum melongena

The deep purple-skinned aubergine is an essential ingredient in many delicious Middle Eastern recipes. It is quite difficult to grow without a greenhouse or polytunnel but if you like a challenge, have a go.

When to Plant

Late spring.

When to Sow

Sow seeds, two each in a 9 cm pot, in mid-spring and keep on a sunny windowsill. Thin to one seedling and keep indoors until all danger of frost has passed. Aubergines need high light intensity to thrive, with a minimum night temperature of 15°C. In early summer plant outside in a sheltered position, spacing them 40 cm apart. Cover with a cloche or polytunnel.

Cultivation

Aubergines require lots of humidity, so place buckets of water between plants to encourage constant evaporation. When they are 25 cm high, nip out the tip of the plant to encourage side shoots to grow. Restrict the fruit to five per plant by removing embryonic fruit as it develops. Once fruit starts to set, feed with an organic tomato fertilizer every 10 days. Keep plants well watered and mulch with straw. Stake tall varieties with canes.

Harvesting & Storing

Pick when the fruit is smooth and plump. They will store in a cool place for a couple of weeks.

Varieties

Black Beauty produces handsome round, black fruit.
Rosa Bianca has attractive globe-shaped fruit and luscious pink flesh.

Pests & Diseases

Aphids, whitefly, red spider mite.

Aubergine and Tomato Bake

Slice 3 medium aubergines lengthways into 5mm–thick slices. Put in a colander and sprinkle with salt, leave for half an hour, rinse and dry. Place on a baking tray, brush generously with olive oil and sprinkle with rosemary. Bake for about 15 mins at 200°C until golden brown.

Make a tomato sauce: heat 75ml of olive oil in a saucepan and fry a medium onion till soft. Add 450g ripe tomatoes and seasoning and simmer gently for 15 mins. Arrange a layer of aubergines in an earthenware dish. Cover with torn up basil leaves and half the tomato sauce. Repeat the layer and sprinkle the top with 110g of grated Parmesan. Bake for 10 mins until bubbling and golden. A delicious supper dish served with salad and hot ciabatta.

BEANS
Phaseolus vulgaris

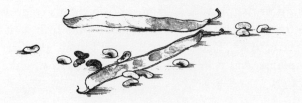

Borlotti, Flageolet and Haricot Beans

These are the beans sold loose in markets in France and Italy. They all have the same requirements, and all are easy to grow. Combined with simple ingredients, they are exceptionally delicious.

Borlotti are the Italian version of the common bean, beautiful to look at with their pale pink skin streaked with maroon and essential in many pasta and soup recipes.

Flageolet and haricot are small white beans that cook to a melting tenderness, absorbing the flavour of other ingredients. The tough outer pod of all these beans allows them to fatten and mature until mid-autumn, to pod or dry for winter use.

When to Sow

Late spring.

Where to Sow

These beans need a light, well-drained soil, rich in organic matter, in the sun. Add compost after you've forked the ground over, and rake it flat. Sow outside, pushing one bean into the ground 5 cm deep, 10 cm between plants, in rows 45 cm apart. Sow extra beans at the end of the row to fill any gaps; or start behind glass in mid-spring, sowing two to a 9 cm pot, and keep on a sunny windowsill. Transplant outside when 10 cm high and when all danger of frost has passed.

Cultivation

Climbing varieties will need supporting on bamboo canes others can be propped up on small sticks to stop them getting muddied (see *Cultivation*, pages 47–51).

Harvesting & Storing

When the pods turn yellow, usually around mid-autumn, pull the entire plant out of the ground and leave on newspaper to go brittle. When dried, these beans have much more flavour than shop-bought ones, and they also freeze brilliantly. Pod the beans and freeze, or when totally dry store in jars—both methods give excellent results.

Varieties
Borlotti Stregonta is fat and fleshy and ideal for freezing.
Borlotto Lini di Nano has an exceptionally good flavour and beautifully mottled red and cream skin.
Chevrier Vert is the classic French flageolet, tasty and tender.
Borlotto Lingua di Fuoco ('Tongue of Fire') is the Italian flageolet frequently found in Italian markets.
Canellino is a large white haricot bean suitable for drying or freezing.
White Soissons is a very old variety of haricot bean with large white pods.

Pests & Diseases
Blackfly, slugs, mice.

Borlotti Beans and Garlic

Soak 450g of borlotti beans overnight. Drain and place in a saucepan and cover with fresh water. Add 2 ripe tomatoes, 6 crushed garlic cloves, 10 sage leaves and 4 tbsps of olive oil. Bring to the boil and skim and simmer for 1–1½ hours until the beans are tender. Season with sea salt and black pepper.

Drain the beans and season to taste. The beans soak up the flavour of the garlic and sage, and are delicious eaten with slow-roasted or grilled meat.

■ ■ ■

BROAD BEANS
Vicia faba

A dish of broad beans glistening with melted butter and chopped mint is a highlight of summer. They are also highly nutritious, being a valuable source of protein.

When to Sow
Mid-spring or early autumn.

Where to Sow
Sow in well-dug soil enriched with manure the season before. Sow single beans in the ground 5 cm deep and 20 cm apart, in double rows 20 cm apart. Sow extra at the end of each row to fill any gaps. Alternatively start behind glass in early spring, putting one seed each in 9 cm pots and planting out when the plant is 10 cm high.

Cultivation
Dwarf varieties do not need support, but tall varieties may lean over. Knock a sturdy post into the ground at each end of the row, tie a length of twine or wire along the row and tie the plants in.

Keep the ground weed-free. If it is very dry when the flowers are forming, give a really good soak to improve the crop. Pinch out the top 10 cm to encourage pods to form.

Harvesting & Storing
Pick the pods when the seeds inside are just showing and are still soft. A surplus can be dried or frozen. Spring-sown seeds will be ready to eat in mid-summer, autumn-sown in spring the following year.

Varieties
Aquadulce is particularly good for autumn or winter sowing to crop in early spring.
Imperial Green Longpod produces dazzling bright green beans and is superb eaten young in salads.

Pests & Diseases
Blackfly, leaf spot, rust, mice.

Broad Bean Purée

Add 1kg of fresh podded broad beans to a pan of unsalted water, bring to the boil and cook for 6 minutes. Drain and put into a food processor with a clove of garlic, squeeze of lemon, 3 tbsps of olive oil and a small bunch of chopped dill. Whizz until smooth, and season with sea salt and black pepper. This Middle Eastern starter is sumptuous served with warm pitta bread.

FRENCH BEANS
Phaseolus vulgaris

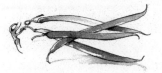

French beans come in a variety of sizes and colours, and all are easy to grow. Be led by what you enjoy eating, and choose from purple, yellow or green, needle-thin or fat and juicy.

When to Plant
Late spring.

Where to Sow
French beans need a light and well-drained soil, rich in organic matter, and sunshine. Add compost after you've forked the ground over and rake it flat. Sow directly in the ground, pushing one bean in 5 cm deep, 23 cm apart, in rows 30 cm apart; or start behind glass in mid-spring, two to a 9 cm pot and keep on a sunny windowsill. Transplant outside when 10 cm high and when all danger of frost has passed. Dwarf varieties can be supported on twiggy cuttings to keep them off the ground. Climbers will need taller supports and both are best installed before planting (see *Cultivation*, pages 47–51).

Cultivation
When climbing beans have reached the top of the cane, pinch out the tip to increase production lower down. Add an organic fertilizer every four weeks. Keep the ground weed-free, and water thoroughly in dry spells.

Harvesting & Storing
Pick regularly to stimulate production. Beans are best eaten fresh but will freeze well.

Varieties
Corona d'Oro has buttery golden pods, is virtually stringless and has an excellent flavour.
Neckar Queen is a prolific climber, producing masses of dark green, pencil pods.

Pests & Diseases
Blackfly, slugs and mice.

Sautéed Beans

The French deal with a glut of beans and lettuce in mid-summer with this delicious recipe. Cook 250g French beans in boiling, salted water until just tender and drain. Melt 25g of butter with a slosh of olive oil in a frying pan. Add a crushed clove of garlic and two small shallots sliced thinly, and fry till golden brown. Add a Cos lettuce sliced lengthways, and cook with the garlic and shallot until the lettuce has wilted. Add the beans and serve hot, seasoned with sea salt and black pepper.

■ ■ ■

RUNNER BEANS
Phaseolus coccineus

Runner beans are one of the most prolific and cost-effective crops to grow. They also look wonderful with their bright red flowers highlighted against dark green leaves.

When to Sow
Late spring.

Where to Sow
They will tolerate part-shade. The ground should be prepared the previous autumn by digging to a spade depth over an area 75 cm wide. Add three to four buckets of well-rotted manure to the area and rake flat. Sow directly in the ground, planting the seeds 5 cm deep, 15 cm apart in double rows 38 cm apart; or start behind glass in mid-spring, one each to a 9 cm pot. Keep on a sunny windowsill and transplant outside when all danger of frost has passed. It is best to erect supports before sowing or planting beans (see *Cultivation*, pages 47–51).

Cultivation
As the beans grow, twine them round supporting sticks, tying them in if necessary. Keep the ground weed-free and water in dry weather. Spray the plants to encourage the flowers to set. When the plant reaches the top of the cane, pinch out the tip to encourage a bushier growth.

Harvesting & Storing
Pick the beans regularly to encourage further cropping. Runner beans can be cut and frozen.

Varieties
White Emergo is a heritage variety producing pretty white flowers followed by tasty, virtually stringless, beans.
Scarlet Emperor produces masses of bright red flowers followed by a heavy crop of very tasty beans.

Pests & Diseases
Blackfly.

Podded Runner Beans
Here's what you do if you have missed a few beans and discovered some as long as your arm. Pop out the fat juicy beans and steam for fifteen minutes until tender. Sprinkle with chopped sage, sea salt, black pepper and a generous dollop of butter. Delicious with grilled fish.

■ ■ ■

BEETROOT
Beta vulgaris

Beetroot is a truly versatile vegetable. Eat it as a small salad root 12–16 weeks after sowing, or leave it to mature in the ground till frosts threaten.

When to Sow
Mid-spring through to late summer.

Where to Sow
Beetroot is greedy, so grow it on soil that has been well manured the previous year. Sow directly in the ground, thinning the seedlings to 11 cm in rows 15 cm apart. Alternatively sow behind glass in biodegradable pots on a sunny windowsill. Sow one seedling per pot and plant out when they are 2.5 cm high. Suppliers offer monogerm seeds that are coated and

bulkier, making them easier to sow and removing the need for thinning.

Cultivation

Water moderately every two weeks and mulch if a dry spell is forecast. Do not over-water, as this will simply produce more leaf. The roots are edible after ten weeks when they can be seen poking through the surface of the ground.

Harvesting & Storing

After pulling beetroots, twist off the foliage leaving 5 cm of stalks. Cutting these off with a knife will result in bleeding, so leave them on for boiling then strip them with the skins. The leaves of small beets can be added to salads, and the leaves of larger crops can be cooked as for chard. Beetroot can be frozen after cooking.

Varieties

Early Wonder has deep red skin and a very sweet flavour.
Monogram has good resistance to bolting and is excellent eaten either as a baby beet or left to mature.

Pests & Diseases

Leaf spot & Downy Mildew.

Roasted Beetroot with Thyme

Fresh thyme combines brilliantly with the sweetness of baby beetroots, and gentle roasting enhances the flavour of both.

Wash 16 baby beetroots and dry. Toss them in a roasting tray with 4 tbsps of olive oil, sea salt, black pepper and a tsp of thyme leaves. Cook at 200°C for 10 minutes, then lower the temperature to 180°C for 30 minutes. Eat hot or cold with crusty French bread.

■ ■ ■

BROCCOLI, PURPLE SPROUTING
Brassica oleracea Italica Group

These delicate-flavoured spears are always expensive to buy. They are easy to grow and provide a delicious early spring vegetable.

When to Sow
Late spring.

Where to Sow
Sow directly in the ground in drills and thin to 60 cm each way. Grow in well-drained soil in a sheltered site in the brassica bed; or start the seeds off behind glass two to a 9 cm pot, thin to one seedling and keep on a sunny windowsill. Plant out when 5 cm tall in late spring.

Cultivation
Keep the ground weed-free. From mid-winter pinch off the main flower head at the top of the plant to encourage sprouting from the sides.

Harvesting & Storing
Keep picking the side shoots to encourage more.

Varieties
Bordeaux can be planted late winter to spring, to crop from mid-summer through to early winter to extend the harvest.
Purple Sprouting Early produces tasty, fat and juicy dark purple spears from a central flower head.

Pests & Diseases
Cabbage root fly, cabbage moth, caterpillars, club root, and pigeons.

Sprouting Broccoli with Aioli

Purple sprouting broccoli is delicious dipped in a garlic mayonnaise. Make the aioli by combining 2 egg yolks, ¼ tsp salt, a pinch of English mustard, 1 crushed garlic clove and 1 dessertspoon of white wine vinegar in a bowl. Drop by drop add 250ml of olive oil, whisking as you do so. As it thickens, add the oil a little faster. Season with sea salt and black pepper. Wash 20 chunky broccoli spears carefully, trim the stalks and any large leaves. Simmer in salted boiling water for 5–7 minutes till just tender. Drain and serve with a bowl of aioli.

BRUSSELS SPROUTS
Brassica oleracea Gemmifera Group

Brussels sprouts are very hardy, surviving the severest weather to provide winter greens.

When to Sow
Early to mid-spring.

Where to Sow
Sow directly in the ground in a seedbed, in drills 1.5 cm deep in rows 15 cm apart. Thin the seedlings to 8 cm apart, and when they are 10 cm high, transplant into the permanent bed. Space 75 cm apart each way and firm the soil to anchor the plant; or sow seeds in 9 cm pots and leave outside in a sheltered spot. Once germinated, thin to one seedling per pot. Keep the compost moist but not sodden.

Cultivation
Keep the ground weed-free. Draw soil around stems 1 month after planting to stabilize. You may need to stake late varieties to keep them upright. Push a wooden batten or thick stick deep in the ground for each plant and make two ties to prevent rocking. Apply a general organic vegetable fertilizer in mid-summer.

Harvesting & Storing
Sowing to harvest time is 14–18 weeks. Harvest sprouts regularly from summer through till spring, using a sharp knife. The leafy tops can be used as spring greens. Sprouts freeze well.

Varieties
Organic Igor F1 produces very delicious sweet-flavoured sprouts. It is resistant to mildew.
Groninger gives a steady supply of sprouts well into winter. Frost improves the flavour.

Pests & Diseases
Caterpillars, cabbage root fly, clubroot, birds.

Frizzled Brussels Sprouts

Here's a new sprout experience that should eradicate any memory of watery offerings forever. Cutting the sprouts lengthways allows you to cook them fast to retain their sweetness.

Cut 450g Brussels sprouts in half and cook in boiling water for 4 minutes till just tender. Drain. Heat 50g butter in a frying pan, add the sprouts and cook till they are golden brown. Season with sea salt and black pepper.

Frizzled sprouts are excellent with roasts or combine with chopped bacon and tagliatelle for a substantial supper dish.

■ ■ ■

CABBAGE FAMILY
Brassica oleracea

CABBAGES

Cabbages come in a variety of colours: reds, grey-green, blue-green, acid-green, all with interesting textured leaves, which range from the heavily veined to blistered and crinkly. If you sow an early, a mid-season and a late variety of cabbage you will get a succession of crops for most of the year. Spring greens are young cabbages that mature in twelve weeks. Plan for a mixture to provide a good selection through the year.

When to Sow
Early spring through to autumn.

Where to Sow
Cabbages are greedy feeders so require a heavily manured brassica bed with a slightly alkaline soil (see *Improving the Soil*, pages 30–37). Sow in a seedbed in drills 1.5 cm deep in rows 15 cm apart. Thin the seedlings to 8 cm apart, and when they are 12 cm tall, transplant into the permanent bed so that the first pair of leaves is level with the soil surface. Space 45 cm apart each way and firm the soil to anchor the plant. Tests show that closer planting (25 cm) gives excellent results. Remember to label each variety if you are sowing for different seasons.

Alternatively sow two seeds each in 9 cm pots early spring and leave outside in a sheltered spot. When germinated, thin to one seedling per pot. Keep the compost moist but not sodden.

Cultivation

Add an organic fertilizer to the surface of the soil around the plants four weeks after planting, watering it in. A large number of pests can affect the cabbage family, so protect the young plants with garden fleece or fine netting.

Harvesting & Storing

Harvest all varieties as soon as the heads are firm—give them a squeeze they should feel good and weighty. Winter cabbages will stand outside until required. Dutch cabbages can be stored in nets or boxes indoors.

Varieties

Winter Cabbages

Marmer Early Red is a dazzling red-purple variety and ideal for pickling.
Jersey Wakefield is an old cultivar with crisp mid-green leaves.

Spring Greens

Pixie is quick to mature, producing delicious tender greens early in the season.
Offenham Compacta is one of the tastiest varieties, with a particularly sweet flavour if cut while still small.

Pests & Diseases

Clubroot, cabbage moth, cabbage root fly, cabbage white caterpillars.

Colcannon

Colcannon came from Ireland in the 18th century. It makes a delicious, inexpensive accompaniment to winter casseroles and stews.

Mash 1kg of cooked potatoes with 50g of butter and 100g of cream. Stir in 350g of cooked, chopped cabbage and 6 chopped spring onions. Season with sea salt and black pepper, and serve piping hot.

CALABRESE
Brassica oleracea Italica Group

Calabrese is a useful late summer vegetable, ready to crop four months after sowing.

When to Sow
Late spring to mid-summer.

Where to Sow
Plant in humus-rich soil in an open sunny spot. Sow directly in the ground, sowing every two weeks in a shallow drill from late spring till mid-summer. Thin the seedlings to 15 cm apart, in rows 30 cm apart.

Calabrese dislikes its roots being disturbed, so alternatively sow in biodegradable pots behind glass in early spring. Sow two seeds per pot and leave the stronger to grow on. Keep on a sunny windowsill until 10 cm high. Plant the whole pot, burying it so that the first set of leaves is touching the soil surface.

Cultivation
Water thoroughly in dry weather, and add a light dressing of an organic nitrogen fertilizer when the young plants have 6–8 leaves. Protect with fleece or fine mesh against cabbage white caterpillars.

Harvesting & Storing
Summer varieties take 16 weeks to mature. Winter varieties will mature up to six months later.

Pick the broccoli-like florets regularly when they are about 15 cm long, to encourage more growth.

Varieties
Waltham produces a central head and numerous side shoots, all with a great flavour.
Fiesta F produces large heads from late summer through to late winter.

Pests & Diseases
Cabbage white caterpillar, club root, pigeons.

Chilli Hot Calabrese

Cut the florets of 450g of calabrese into small clusters and cook in boiling salted water for 5–6 minutes, drain and keep hot. In a frying pan, heat 3 tbsps of olive oil, add 2 cloves of crushed garlic and 1 red chilli chopped and seeded. Allow to sizzle and pour over the calabrese. Season with sea salt and black pepper.

■ ■ ■

CARROTS
Daucus carota

The taste of fresh carrots is incomparably better than the supermarket offerings. Pick them whilst they are young and sweet.

When to Sow
Early spring to early summer.

Where to Sow
Carrots hate freshly manured ground and require a deep, well-worked soil, free from stones.

Sow directly in the ground, aiming for one plant every 4–5 cm along the row with 15 cm between rows. Carrot fly attack can be a problem. The fly is attracted to the smell of the leaves when thinning out, so if possible thin out in the evening. Some growers leave sowing until after mid-summer when the carrot fly has died out.

Cultivation
A fleece cover will help to protect against carrot fly. Water regularly in the first six weeks after the carrot tops emerge. Once established, avoid watering unless the weather is exceptionally dry.

Harvesting & Storing
Baby carrots will be ready about 7 weeks after sowing, and the main crop after about 4 months. To store carrots, cut the tops off just above the root and layer in wooden boxes in slightly moist sand. Keep in a cool shed until required.

Varieties

Carrots, like potatoes, come in a huge variety of shapes and subtly different flavours. Study the seed catalogues and experiment with early, main and late varieties.

Chantenay is an early variety. You can be washing them under the allotment tap and eating them after only 51 days.

Fly Away F1 has two advantages. It has been bred for carrot fly resistance and has a delicious flavour.

Pests & Diseases

Carrot fly.

Turkish Carrot Salad

Peel and wash 500g carrots and grate on a coarse grater. Heat 5 tbsps oil in a frying pan, add the carrots and 2 cloves of crushed garlic and cook over a gentle heat for 10 minutes. Cool and add to 300ml of natural yoghurt. Season with sea salt and black pepper, and sprinkle with a handful of chopped mint.

■ ■ ■

CAULIFLOWERS
Brassica oleracea Botrytis Group

Cauliflowers can be quite tricky to grow, being the greediest of all the brassicas. You may like to experiment by planting them close together to crop them when the heads are small.

When to Sow

Early to mid-spring for summer and autumn crops, late spring for winter cropping types.

Where to Sow

Before buying seed, think about when you want to harvest and choose accordingly. Purchase seedling plants or sow two seeds in 9 cm pots indoors or in a cold frame. Thin to one seedling and keep well watered.

Cultivation

Cauliflowers are greedy feeders, so add lots of well-rotted organic matter to the soil before planting. Plant out as soon as the seedlings have reached 10 cm. Space 15 cms each way for baby cauliflowers and 45 cm each way for standard heads. Never let cauliflowers dry out—they like lots of water. Feed regularly with an organic fertilizer. Cover with a fleece to protect from pests.

Harvesting & Storing

Baby cauliflowers take ten weeks to mature; full size cauliflowers will take up to 32 weeks. They can be stored for a few weeks in a shed with their roots on, or the florets can be frozen.

Varieties

Purple Cape is a dramatic purple variety that grows quickly for an autumn crop.

Snowball is an over wintering type with a large cream head and delicate flavour.

Pests & Diseases

Cabbage root fly, cabbage white caterpillars, cabbage white butterflies, clubroot disease.

Spicy Potato and Cauliflower

Break off the florets from a cauliflower and cook for 4 minutes. Peel 450g of small new potatoes and boil till tender. Drain both the vegetables, put into a salad bowl and season with sea salt. Mix 1 tsp of harissa paste, and 1 tsp of ground cumin with 4 tbsps of olive oil, half a lemon and 2 tbsps of chopped parsley. Pour onto the vegetables and toss them gently to cover.

CELERIAC
Apim graveolens

Celeriac is a delicious root vegetable, but fairly expensive to buy. It is relatively easy to grow, and has a celery-like flavour and texture like parsnips when cooked.

When to Sow
Mid-spring.

Where to Sow
Celeriac requires rich soil in full sun. Sow in seed trays behind glass; germination is often erratic, so be patient. Keep on a sunny windowsill, then when the seedlings are big enough to handle, prick out individually into 9 cm pots. Harden off in a cold frame during the day. Plant out in late spring 30 cm apart both ways.

Cultivation
Water well throughout the growing season, and give an organic vegetable feed from time to time.

Harvesting & Storing
Leave in the ground till required, covering with fleece or hessian if frost is forecast. Roots can be stored in boxes of moist sand in a cool shed.

Varieties
Prinz produces smooth round roots making it easy to peel.
President has a crisp white flesh with an excellent flavour for grating raw in salad.

Pests & Diseases
Celery fly and slugs.

Celeriac Mash

Peel 500g each of potatoes and celeriac. Chop up and boil in salted water, until tender. Mash with 50g of butter and add 50g cream. Season with sea salt & black pepper. Delicious with pork or game.

CELERY
Apium graveolens var. dolce

Celery is traditionally grown in trenches and needs earthing up to produce edible heads. The self-blanching varieties avoid this and are relatively easy to grow.

When to Sow
Early spring.

Where to Sow
Self-blanching celery needs a well-dug soil rich in organic matter. Sow the seeds (probably the tiniest of any crop) behind glass in seed trays as thinly as possible. The seeds can take up to three weeks to germinate, and need to be in the warm on a sunny windowsill. Use a fine mist spray daily to keep them moist. When the seedlings have six leaves, prick out one each into 9 cm pots. Harden off in a cold frame outside during the day. Do not let the seedlings dry out; the key to successful celery is water at all stages. Plant out in early summer 23 cm apart.

Cultivation
Celery needs high nitrogen levels, so every few weeks give an organic liquid feed to the soil at the base of the plant. Self-blanching varieties of celery will be made even sweeter if a piece of heavy brown paper is tied around each plant when they are 30–38 cm high. Repeat as the stems grow, every 4 weeks.

Harvesting & Storing
Celery will be ready to harvest 16–18 weeks after planting and will stand in the ground till frost threatens. Lift with the roots and store upright in a box of moist sand in a cool shed.

Varieties
Golden Self-Blanching produces crisp and tasty stems.
Solid Pink is an old cultivar with red-washed stems that retain their colour when cooked.

Pests & Diseases
Celery fly, carrot fly and slugs.

Celery Soup

Cut a head of celery into 1.25 cm chunks, wash thoroughly and put in a pan with a quartered onion. Cover with 1 litre of vegetable stock. Cook for about 20 mins until tender. Scoop out the celery and onion, and purée with 100ml of cream and 1 tbsp of chopped lovage leaves. Return to the stock, and season with sea salt and black pepper.

■ ■ ■

CHICORY & RADICCHIO
Cichorium intybus

Chicory leaves picked young are often included in those delicious bags of Italian salad leaves found in supermarkets. They are easy to grow and very robust, so are particularly useful for winter salads. The leaves of chicory turn red as the temperature drops, and are often called Radicchio.

When to Sow
Mid-spring through to late summer.

Where to Sow
Sow in fertile well-drained soil in sun or part shade. Sow thinly directly in the ground in a drill. Water regularly. Thin to 20 cm when the first leaves start to appear.

Space all chicory types 25 cm apart if you want fat heads, or closer for cut-and come-again salad leaf pickings.

Cultivation
Water sparingly to encourage root growth. Tying up with twine will encourage plump blanched heads. The natural growing season for chicory is from summer to early winter, but covering with a cloche or fleece will extend the season.

Harvesting & Storing
Crops sown in mid-spring will be ready in early summer. Mid-summer sown crops will be ready in autumn. Pick the leaves from the main

plant to encourage more, or leave to grow into a fatter head. If the chicory is too bitter, soak it in cold water for 30 mins before using.

Varieties
Grumolo Verde produces early leaves for salads and more substantial heads for winter.
Rossa di Treviso is a variegated variety, starting off green and turning red in winter.

Pests & Diseases
Slugs.

Grilled Chicory or Radicchio

Take 4 plump heads, discard any damaged leaves, and wash if necessary. Cut in half lengthways, cutting into the root part so that the oil can penetrate. Place on a grill pan and brush with olive oil. Sprinkle with sea salt and black pepper. Put under a hot grill about 10 cm from the heat. After 7 minutes turn the chicory over and brush with more olive oil. Cook for a further 7 minutes then baste with the oil in the pan, adding more if necessary. Cook for another 8 minutes, by which time it will look slightly charred. Delicious with griddled tuna or chicken.

■　■　■

COURGETTES
Cucurbita pepo

Courgettes are the young, immature fruit of marrows (or summer squash). Their skins vary in colour from dark green to yellow or striped. Prolific croppers, they can produce up to twenty courgettes on each plant.

When to Plant
Early summer.

Where to Sow
Courgettes do best in a sunny position but will tolerate some shade. They are very hungry feeders, and can be planted on an old heap of

well-rotted manure or compost provided you will not need it before the autumn. Start the seeds off, one each in 9 cm pots on a sunny windowsill four weeks before you want to plant. Prepare a planting hole 30 cms deep and fork in some well-rotted manure or garden compost. Water the hole, tap the courgette plant out of its pot and plant it firming the soil around it. Space the plants 90 cm apart. Mulch with straw to keep weeds down.

Cultivation
Give them a good soaking once a week at ground level. A liquid organic feed will assist the fruiting once the flowers appear. Courgettes produce male and female flowers and are fertilized by insects carrying the pollen between plants. In dull or wet weather this may not happen, in which case use a soft brush to transfer the pollen from the male to the female flower. An embryo fruit behind the flower distinguishes the female from the male, which has no fruit.

Harvesting & Storing
Cut the fruit from the plant with a sharp knife, as twisting the fruit off may lift the plant out of the soil at the roots. Pick when they are young and about 10–13 cm long. The more you pick, the more the plant will produce. Courgettes keep for about a week.

Varieties
Defender produces dark green, heavy yields, all summer long. It is also virus-resistant.
Genovese has bright green fruit and large orange flowers, perfect for shredding and adding to salads.

Pests & Diseases
Slugs, aphids, mildew, mosaic virus.

Marrow and Ginger Jam

If your courgettes turn to marrows (it can happen in a matter of days) comfort yourself by making this delicious jam.

Peel 3kg of marrows and remove the seeds; cut the flesh into tiny cubes and steam until tender. Peel and chop 60g of root ginger and tie in a muslin bag. Put in a saucepan with the steamed marrow and the grated rind and juice of 4 lemons. Add 3kg of sugar, stirring until the sugar has dissolved, and then boil rapidly to setting point. Test for setting by spooning a little jam on to a cold saucer. If ready, a skin will form on the surface and will wrinkle when pushed. Pot at once.

FLORENCE FENNEL
Foeniculum vulgare var. dulce

Fennel is a beautiful, feathery-leaved vegetable grown for the crisp, aniseed-flavoured bulb. It is also an aphid repellant.

When to Sow
Early summer to late summer.

Where to Sow
Fennel needs well-drained, moisture-retentive soil, rich in organic matter. From early summer onwards you can sow directly in the ground, thinning plants to 30 cm each way. Alternatively sow seed in biodegradable pots behind glass in early spring. This reduces the risk of bolting, which is triggered by transplanting. Keep on a sunny windowsill and plant out when four leaves are visible, spacing as above.

Cultivation
Keep weeded, water regularly and mulch with garden compost at the base of the plant. Cover with a cloche or fleece if frost threatens in autumn.

Harvesting & Storing
Plants mature in about 12 weeks. Cut the bulb at least 2.5 cm above soil level but leave the root in the ground. It should re-sprout, producing small but tasty shoots that are excellent in salads.

Varieties
Argo is particularly vigorous and resistant to bolting.
Romanesco produces lovely feathery foliage from big white bulbs that weigh up to a kg.

Pests & Diseases
Slugs may attack young plants.

Fennel and Parsnip Soup

Melt 50g of butter in a soup pan and toss in 225g each of diced parsnip and fennel, and a medium-size chopped onion. Cover and cook on a gentle heat for 15 minutes. Add 1 litre of chicken or vegetable stock and cook until the vegetables are tender, about 30 mins. Cool and liquidize, then add 125ml of cream. Season with sea salt and black pepper. Sprinkle on some chopped fennel leaves.

■ ■ ■

GARLIC
Allium sativum

Garlic helps to maintain a healthy immune system. It was fed to Egyptian slaves to keep then fit whilst building the pyramids. The scent of garlic leaves is believed to repel aphids.

When to Plant
Spring or autumn.

Where to Sow
Garlic is easy to grow in a weed-free, sunny bed in any well-drained soil in prepared ground. Buy bulbs from a garden centre or seed supplier, as you get better results than by using garlic from the supermarket. Separate the cloves and push into the soil 3 cm deep, with the pointed tip uppermost. Leave 10–20 cm between bulbs, depending on size of the garlic.

Cultivation
If birds pull the green shoots out of the soil, make a space with a trowel and push them back in. Keep the ground weed-free.

Harvesting & Storing
When the leaves start to turn yellow and die down, lift the bulbs with a fork and dry on the soil surface in the sun. When dry, cut off the roots and leave the grassy tops for plaiting or tying together in bunches. Garlic planted in autumn matures at the same time as spring-planted bulbs, generally mid-to late summer, and will keep for about a year stored in the dry.

Varieties
Thermidrome is especially suited to autumn planting.
Printanor is a trouble-free variety for spring planting.

Pests & Diseases
Rust.

Roasted Garlic and Potatoes

Scrub 4 large 'old potatoes', leaving the skin on, and cut into eighths lengthways. Put into a roasting tin, drizzle with olive oil and toss so that they are lightly coated. Roast in the oven at 200°C. After 30 minutes add 12 or more whole cloves of garlic. Roast for about 30 minutes more, keeping an eye on the garlic— it should be soft in the middle but not burnt. If necessary, take it out and keep warm until the potatoes are golden and crisp. Press the creamy, sweet garlic out of the skins and eat with the potatoes.

■　■　■

GLOBE ARTICHOKES
Cynara scolymus Scolymus Group

These make a dramatic statement on the allotment: their beautiful silver leaves can reach up to 1.5 metres, and as a perennial, globe artichokes will return year after year.

When to Plant
Mid-spring.

Where to Sow
Sow seed in a tray in late winter on a sunny windowsill. When four leaves are visible, prick out the strongest seedlings into individual 9 cm pots and grow on till mid-spring. Harden off by putting the pots outside for a few hours daily to prepare them for life in the ground. Plant out when 10 cm high in a sunny sheltered site in very rich soil. Allow at least 75 cm between plants, and keep well watered.

Cultivation
Globe artichokes benefit from a mulch of garden compost in spring plus a liquid feed throughout the growing season. The spectacular flower buds will begin to appear in early summer, and the plants may produce as many as twelve artichokes. In the first year the flowers can be picked off so that the energy goes into putting down deep roots

rather than producing edible heads. Cut down the entire plant in early winter and protect the crowns in frosty weather with fleece or straw.

Harvesting & Storing
They are ready to harvest when the outer scales have opened flat, and should be cut from the main stem leaving a short stalk. They will store in a dry place for up to two weeks.

Varieties
Green Globe is one of the most reliable varieties, producing tight heads on stems up to 1.2 metres.
Purple Globe-Romanesco has delicately tinted red-tinged scales and a fine flavour.

Pests & Diseases
Globe artichokes generally remain free of trouble, but look out for slugs hidden in the mulch in spring.

Globe Artichokes with Melted Butter

Add 2 tsp each of salt and white wine vinegar to a pan of water and simmer the artichokes whole for about 30 minutes, until the scales are tender. The best part is the fleshy base under the bud or 'choke'. Pull off each scale and dip in melted butter.

■ ■ ■

JERUSALEM ARTICHOKES
Helianthus tuberosus

Jerusalem artichokes are like small, knobbly potatoes with a delectable sweet flavour.

When to Plant
Early spring.

Where to Sow
Purchase the small tubers in late winter. Plant them 10–15 cm deep and 30 cm apart in any soil in an open position in early spring. Artichokes can become invasive, so you may wish to contain them in a raised bed.

Cultivation

The leafy foliage will reach 1.8 metres high and may need staking against high winds. Remove any flower buds that develop. In late summer, pinch the top of the plants off to inhibit growth. In autumn, as the leaves blacken, cut back to ground level. In severe frost, protect with a cloche or mulch with straw. Mark the rows to find the roots for cropping later.

Harvesting & Storing

Dig up from early winter through till spring as needed. It is essential to remove all the roots from the ground or they will spread and produce weak artichokes the following year. Save some good tubers to re-plant next year. Store all artichokes in a dry frost-free shed.

Varieties

Fuseau (non-organic) has a wonderful smoky flavour with a smooth skin, making it easy to prepare.

Pests & Diseases

Jerusalem artichokes will generally remain free of trouble.

Jerusalem Artichokes with Parsley and Pancetta

Melt 50g of butter in a large pan and add 450g of scrubbed and halved Jerusalem artichokes. Add 30g of chopped pancetta and fry for 4 minutes. Add 100ml of water, put the lid on and cook very slowly for 30–45 minutes until just tender. Check that they do not dry out and add a small amount of water if necessary. Taste and season with sea salt, black pepper and sprinkle with chopped parsley.

KALE
Brassica oleracea Acephala Group

Kale is an ideal vegetable for winter greens. It is extremely hardy, and produces an abundance of tender, dramatic foliage. It needs space but is an ideal crop to follow on from the last of the peas harvested in mid-summer.

When to Sow
Mid-summer.

Where to Sow
Sow the seeds thinly in a seedbed in the ground 1 cm deep and thin to 10 cm apart when they are 5 cm tall. Transplant to final site in mid-summer, planting 45 cm apart. If you are waiting for space, sow two seeds each in 9 cm pots outside and keep watered until ready to plant.

Cultivation
Water regularly throughout the summer.

Harvesting & Storing
The first young leaves will be ready to pick from early winter through to early spring.

Varieties
Westland Winter produces densely curled blue-green leaves and a long harvesting period.
Cavolo Nero di Toscana is an Italian curly kale with handsome purple-green leaves.

Pests & Diseases
Clubroot, cabbage root fly, cabbage moth, cabbage butterflies, birds.

Ribollita

Heat 2 tbsps of oil in a large saucepan. Chop 1 red onion, 4 celery stalks, 120g carrots, 2 cloves of garlic and add to the pan. Cook over a gentle heat for 20 mins. Add 225g of chopped, skinned tomatoes and cook for a further 20 mins. Add 500g of chopped Cavolo Nero and 125g of cooked borlotti beans and cover with 500ml of water. Simmer for 30 mins, then add half a medium loaf of stale ciabatta torn into pieces. Season with sea salt and black pepper, and a handful of chopped flat-leaf parsley. This famous Italian soup should be served just as it is, steaming hot.

KOHLRABI
Brassica oleracea Gongolydes Group

Kohlrabi is an odd-looking vegetable producing kale-like, edible leaves from a root the size of a tennis ball. The root has a nutty, fresh flavour and should be cooked like a turnip.

When to Sow
Early spring through to late summer.

Where to Sow
A member of the brassica family, it tolerates drought but should be grown on adequately limed soil. Sow seeds in drills 2 cm deep in the brassica bed and repeat the sowing every two weeks for a continuous supply. Thin the plants when they are large enough to handle, spacing them 10 cm apart in rows about 30 cm apart. It is worth growing as a catch crop as it matures in just 8–10 weeks.

Cultivation
Mulching with compost encourages fast growth.

Harvesting & Storing
Pull up when the roots are about 5 cm in diameter, as you need them. Late sowings can be harvested before the threat of frost and stored in boxes in layers of sand.

Varieties
Olivia is slow to bolt, so is good for sowing early to extend the season. *Azur Star* has striking deep purple skin and sweet white flesh.

Pests & Diseases
Slugs and flea beetle.

Sautéed Kohlrabi

Wash and peel 450g of kohlrabi and cut into 5mm slices. Melt 30g of butter in a cast iron saucepan, and add the kohlrabi plus 1 tbsp of chopped marjoram. Season with sea salt and black pepper, put the lid on and simmer very gently until just tender—about 10 minutes. This dish is particularly delicious with game.

LEEKS
Allium porrum

Rather like onions, you can't have too many leeks as they are endlessly versatile and easy to store.

When to Sow
Mid-spring to mid-summer.

Where to Sow
Leeks are easy to grow in any well-drained soil. Fork a general organic fertilizer into the bed and give the ground a thorough soaking a week before planting. Sow in the seedbed from mid-spring in drills 2 cm deep and transplant the seedlings when they are 20 cm tall, 15 cm apart with 30 cm between rows. Make planting holes 15 cm deep with a trowel and drop the leeks in. Fill the hole with water; this will bring some earth with it. The aim is to allow the long roots of leeks lots of space to develop without compacting the earth too much around the roots. Draw the soil up around the neck of the plants to support them and to encourage longer blanched stems. Seed should be sown in early spring for autumn leeks, and late spring for winter leeks that will be cropped till the following spring.

If you are waiting for the ground to be empty from a previous crop you can sow seeds indoors from early spring onwards. Re-usable plastic modules are useful if you want to grow lots of leeks; some take up to 140 seeds. Sow sparely in moist compost and thin to one seed each module. Push the plug out, and pot on to 9 cm pots when there is 8 cm of leaf. Keep behind glass in temperatures not less than 15°C. Place outdoors for a few hours daily to harden off from mid-spring onwards—they take 10–15 weeks to reach a size for planting out.

Baby Leeks
Sow short rows from spring through to mid-summer in drills 15 cm apart. Thin the seedlings to about 2 cm apart and water regularly. They can be pulled after 13 weeks, when they will have grown into tender young plants measuring 15–20 cm.

Cultivation

Water gently every day if the weather is dry until the plants are established. Earth up the stems to increase blanching. If worms push them out after planting, simply re-plant.

Harvesting & Storing

The time from sowing to harvest is flexible since the crop can be left in the ground till required, but expect about 30–40 weeks from a spring sowing to a final cropping.

Varieties

Hannibal is a heavy yielding autumn crop good for extending the season. *St Victor* is an excellent late variety with stunning blue-purple leaves. It will stay in the ground till late spring.

Pests & Diseases

Onion fly, rust.

Leek and Butter Beans

Soak 250g of butter beans overnight. Drain, cover with water and simmer for 1–1½ hours till tender. Heat 50g of butter and 2 tbsps of olive oil in a heavy saucepan. When the butter is bubbling, add 3 finely sliced medium-size leeks. Cook until soft about 20 minutes, drain the beans and add to the leeks. Season with sea salt and black pepper and sprinkle with chopped chives. These are delicious served with roasts.

■ ■ ■

LETTUCE AND SALAD LEAVES

The salad section in all the seed catalogues offers a huge variety of interesting lettuces and leaves. Try the 'cut and come again' cultivars— pick the leaves from a central stem as you need them, or the whole head types ('crispheads'), which form tight balls of crisp leaves, or the Cos types, tall and pointed.

Experiment with different salad leaves: some seed suppliers offer packets of mixed seeds for different seasons. This is a good opportunity to taste a variety of spicy, sweet and mustard flavoured leaves from one sowing. With a range of varieties, you will be able to harvest in spring, summer and winter and save a fortune in bought packets of leaves.

LETTUCES
Lactuca sativa

When to Sow
Mid-spring to early autumn.

Where to Sow
Lettuces will tolerate some shade; plant in any spare space in reasonably rich, moisture-retentive ground. Sow seeds in a drill 1 cm deep and thin out to 15–20 cm between upright lettuces and 30–35 cm between crispheads in rows 30 cm apart. Sow seed every two weeks from mid-spring to guarantee a good supply.

Alternatively, sow behind glass in early spring in pots or seed trays, ready to plant out in mid-spring. For a winter supply, sow behind glass in late summer to plant out in the autumn.

Cultivation
An organic liquid feed once a fortnight plus regular watering will encourage growth of leaves. Avoid sowing in the heat of mid-summer, as the seed will remain dormant in very hot weather. Provide some shelter in winter either with cloches, small polytunnels or fleece.

Harvesting & Storing
Pick 'cut and come again' varieties regularly to encourage new growth. Cut crispheads just above ground to encourage re-growth of leaves from the base. Pick whole head lettuces as soon as the heads feel firm.

Varieties
Saladin is a crisphead with a sweet flavour and crunchy texture that keeps well in the fridge.
Sherwood is a Cos type with a crisp texture and a sweet flavour, and with good mildew resistance.
Little Gem is a small Cos lettuce, perfect as a catch crop or as an early sowing variety.
Oakleaf is a large loose-leaf type with densely lobed leaves tinted with red.
Red Salad Bowl is a cut-and-come again type with long indented red leaves.

Pests & Diseases
Slugs, downy mildew.

SALAD LEAVES

When to Sow
Mid-spring to early autumn.

Where to Sow
Prepare the ground as for lettuces and sow seeds directly in the ground.

Cultivation
Keep well watered and give an organic feed once a month.

Harvesting & Storing
Cut the leaves with scissors when they are about 10 cm, leaving the cut stump. Within a few weeks a fresh crop of leaves will have grown.

Varieties
Lambs Lettuce (Valerianella locusta) is sometimes known as corn salad. It has a mild, nutty taste, and a long sowing and harvesting period. Sow as for lettuce, and thin plants to 10 cm in rows 15 cm apart. It is ideal for winter salads if sown in late summer for autumn/winter cropping.
Rocket (Erica sativa) is a highly spiced salad leaf. Sow seed directly in the ground, thinning to 15 cm apart. Pick regularly when the seedlings are 5 cm tall. Repeat sow every few weeks. Rocket flowers are edible.
Eruca vesicaria is known as wild rocket. It lasts longer before running to seed so is worth looking for in seed catalogues.

The following mixed packets are good to experiment with:
Summer Mixed Leaves will contain a mix of Pak Choi, Mizuna, Mustard Tai Ping Po, Rocket, Tatsai and Italian dandelion Red Rib. Sow directly in ground from late spring to late summer.
Autumn Mixed Leaves will contain a mix of Choy Sum, Tatsai, Greek Cress, Mustard Suehlihung, Rocket and Lovely Choi. Sow directly in ground in late summer/early autumn. A cloche will protect the leaves from severe winter weather.

Pests & Diseases
Slugs, downy mildew.

Warm Salad with Goats Cheese

Pick a selection of lettuce, salad leaves, radicchio, rocket and flat leaf parsley. Wash and dry the leaves, tearing the larger ones into bite-size pieces. Make a dressing: combine 2 tbsps each of walnut oil, olive oil, white wine vinegar, a dash of French mustard, sea salt and black pepper. Slice a fresh goat's cheese weighing 225g into 8 and sit on top of 8 slices of toasted French bread. Put under a hot grill until soft and golden then place on top of the lightly dressed leaves.

■ ■ ■

ONIONS & SHALLOTS
Allium cepa

Onions are infinitely versatile as a vegetable, and the leaves are said to repel aphids. They are easy to grow and keep for months, so plant lots.

When to Plant
Spring and autumn.

Where to Sow
Onions like sun and free-draining soil that has been dug over and raked flat. Aim for a loose texture—too firm and the roots will push the onion out of the ground. Do not plant on freshly manured soil, as onions prefer ground that has been heavily manured the year before.

Buy onion sets—immature bulbs which have been specially grown for planting. The advantage over onion seeds is that they mature quicker and are not attacked by mildew or onion fly. Japanese and European autumn varieties can be planted in early autumn and main crop ones in spring.

Shallots are also grown from sets, and grow fast to produce a cluster of bulbs in summer. The green leaves can be chopped up for salads. Plant shallots 15 cm apart in rows 18 cm apart.

Salad onions need the same soil conditions as onions and shallots. Make small successive sowings at three-week intervals, thinning to 4 cm apart in rows 10 cm apart.

Plant onion bulbs 11 cm apart in rows 10 cm apart. A closer planting works well, but the onions will be smaller. Push the bulb gently into the soil so that the tip is level with the surface.

Cultivation

Cover with netting if birds are a problem, and keep the bed weed-free—
onions hate competition! If birds or frost lift them out of the soil, make
a hole with a trowel and push back in. In most years, neither onions
nor shallots will need extra watering, but you can increase the yield of
shallots by giving a soaking about two months after planting when the
bulb is just beginning to swell.

Harvesting & Storing

Harvest shallots and onions when the leaves have turned yellow by lifting them with a fork. Leave on the surface of the soil to dry out, sepa-
rating each bulb of shallots. Autumn-sown sets mature in early summer,
spring planted sets in 18–20 weeks. Drying out will take about three
weeks, depending on size. If rain is forecast, rub off any soil, discard
any damaged bulbs and dry them indoors strewn on newspaper. Store
in net bags or trays, or plait them into a rope.

Varieties

Onions

Red Baron has a shiny dark red skin and a delicious sweet flavour.
Dorato di Parma produces a mild-flavoured bulb and stores well.

Shallots

Mikor has red-golden skin with delicate pink-tinged flesh.
Longor is a traditional French shallot with yellow skin and a strong
flavour.

Salad Onions

White Lisbon Winter Hardy can be sown in autumn and harvested in
spring.
Ramrod produces strong, long white stems, excellent for shredding in
stir fry.

Pests & Diseases

Onion fly, downy mildew.

Champ

*Mash 1 kg of cooked potatoes with 75g of butter. Chop 8 spring
onions and 3 tbsps of flat leaf parsley, and add to the mash with
sea salt and black pepper. Serve piping hot with rich casseroles.*

ORIENTAL GREENS

Chinese cabbage has been known in China and parts of Asia since the 5th century. Now a favourite ingredient in European cooking, it is easy to grow, as are a host of other undemanding oriental vegetables—pak choi, mustards and Japanese Greens.

When to Sow
Early summer.

Where to Sow
Choose an open site with very fertile, moisture-retentive soil and sow seed directly in the ground. Thin Chinese cabbbage and larger types of oriental greens to 30–38 cm each way to produce heads. Pak choi can be thinned to 23 cm each, and mustards and greens can be thinned to an even closer spacing of 10–15 cm. Alternatively sow seeds thinly, preferably in biodegradable pots to reduce root disturbance, in late spring behind glass. Any earlier, the risk of a sudden drop in temperature will cause the plants to bolt and produce flower heads. Thin to 1 seedling per pot. Gradually harden off in partial shade, keep well watered and watch out for slugs.

Cultivation
Mulch with compost to conserve moisture and to keep the bed weed-free. Be prepared to water frequently, as Chinese cabbages have very shallow roots. Add an organic fertilizer as a surface feed every four weeks. Tie the leaves with raffia as the Chinese cabbage begins to form a heart. If you use a cloche or polytunnel, *Mizuna*, *Green in Snow* and *Tat Soi* can be sown in late August for a winter harvest that will go on till spring. In summer you may need to protect the greens with fine mesh or fleece covers against pests.

Harvesting & Storing
Cut Chinese cabbages leaving a stump—this will produce new leaves. Younger leaves of all oriental greens can be used as salad leaves and older leaves used in stir-fry or steamed.

Varieties

Chinese Cabbage (Brassica rapa Pekinensis Group)

Wongbok produces a dense, mid-green head with a mild flavour and crunchy texture.

Tat Soi is a loose-leaved type with light green, round leaves that can be harvested five weeks after sowing.

Pak Choi (Brassica rapa Chinensis Group)

China Choi is a reliable variety slow to bolt.

Canton Dwarf produces glossy green leaves that melt like spinach when cooked, whilst the thick white stems remain crunchy like bean shoots.

Oriental Mustards (Brassica juncea)

Mustards have a hot flavour, so pick the leaves small for salads or when mature for stir-fry.

Red Giant has very decorative green leaves, mottled red.

Green in Snow is very hardy so will make a winter green if re-sown in late August.

Japanese Greens (Brassica rapa var. nipposinica)

Mizuna forms clumps of feathery dissected leaves and will be ready to eat three-four weeks from sowing.

Green Boy is another vigorous plant, maturing in thirty-five days in summer.

Pests & Diseases

Slugs, cabbage root fly, cabbage white butterfly.

Pak Choi with Ginger and Tomatoes

Cut 450g of pak choi into 2 cm slices and steam until tender—about 3 minutes. Heat 2 tbsps of oil till hot in a wok, add 1 tsp each of grated ginger and garlic, and 2 skinned and chopped tomatoes. Cook for 1–2 minutes, then add the steamed pak choi, tossing together for 30 seconds. Add chopped spring onions, season with sea salt and black pepper, and serve with buttered noodles.

PARSNIPS
Pastinaca sativa

Parsnips are delicious eaten as a baby vegetable in summer, or left in the ground until you are ready to eat them in winter.

When to Sow
Late spring.

Where to Sow
Parsnips do best in a slightly acid soil (pH 6.5), and ideally in a bed that was manured for a previous crop. So they are grouped with onions in the crop rotation plan, to follow in the bed used for last year's heavily manured brassica crops. They require a deep, well-worked soil, free from stones. Warm the soil with a cloche or fleece prior to sowing. Reduce the need to thin out by sowing sparingly, directly into the ground, in late spring. Sow a couple of seeds every 15 cm across the patch and leave 30 cm between rows. If you are growing baby parsnips, space the seeds every 5 cm and leave 15 cm between rows. If you are waiting for ground to be free, then sow in 9 cm pots behind glass in spring or in a cold frame in summer. Thin to one plant per pot, keep well-watered and plant in the ground by mid-summer.

Cultivation
The seed is notoriously erratic, so you may not see results for a number of weeks. Sow a fast-growing radish in the same drill as a marker. The radish will have cropped before the parsnip needs the space, and the leaf is sufficiently different for it to be easy to identify. Sow every two weeks for a regular supply, and be vigilant with weed control. Water the young plants regularly in summer but winter plants will need little attention. Frosts are said to enhance the flavour.

Harvesting & Storing
Parsnips take from 17 weeks to mature and can be left in the ground until needed. The tops will die down, so mark the row to find them in snow. Alternatively lift and store in boxes of sand.

Varieties

Tender and True is an old variety with a good flavour.
Turga has a smooth skin and lovely creamy texture, making it ideal for purées.

Pests & Diseases

Carrot fly, celery fly.

Roasted Root Vegetables

Pre-heat the oven to 200°C. Chop into 4 cm chunks, 6 each of carrots, parsnips and medium-size red onions. Place in a large bowl and drizzle on 50g of olive oil, sea salt and black pepper. Spread in a single layer in a roasting tin and roast until fully cooked about 30 mins. Be vigilant: they should be caramelized, not burnt. Serve sprinkled with chopped thyme, parsley or rosemary.

■ ■ ■

PEAS, MANGE TOUT & SUGAR SNAP
Pisum sativum

Fresh garden peas are one of the highlights of summer—even shelling them is a pleasure. Mange tout and sugar snap peas produce edible pods.

When to Sow

Early spring through to late autumn.

Where to Sow

All require very rich, deeply worked soil with good drainage in the sun. Sow directly in the ground in shallow trenches 18 cm wide, and about 5 cm deep, scattering the peas evenly. Rows should be 60 cm apart and seedlings thinned to one plant every 10 cm.

Cultivation

Support peas on twiggy branches (see *Cultivation*, pages 47–51). Alternatively knock in substantial posts at either end of the row with a couple in the middle and secure netting across the row. It is best to put supports in place before or shortly after seedlings emerge. If severe weather is forecast, cover with a cloche or fleece.

Harvesting & Storing

All peas, sugar snap and mange tout should be picked regularly to encourage more pods. Peas are best cooked within 30 minutes of picking. Harvest mange tout and sugar snap peas when the peas are very small. They have a crunchy texture and a sweet flavour, and can be stir-fried, steamed or eaten raw in salads. Podded peas, sugar snap and mange tout can all be frozen.

Varieties

Peas
Karina is sweet tasting and early.
Kelvedon Wonder is quick maturing and needs minimum support.

Mange Tout
Weggisser is an old Swiss variety with a superb sweet flavour.
Norli produces a profusion of disease-resistant pods, and is perfect uncooked in salads.

Sugar Snap
Sugar Snap has a succulent, sweet pod and is a heavy cropper.
Sugar Pea Dwarf Sweet Green produces crops of flat, stringless pods over a long period.

Asparagus Pea
This has the texture of a mange tout and the flavour of asparagus—sweet and crisp. It grows as a low bush covered in red pea-like flowers. Sow as for mange tout and sugar snap. There are no named varieties.

Pests & Diseases
Pea and bean weevil, leaf spot, pea moth.

Pea Soup

This is a simply delicious summer treat. If you have a bumper crop of peas you can freeze the soup and add the cream when reheating. Boil 450g peas, 1 small chopped onion and 1 medium chopped potato in a litre of stock until soft. Scoop out the cooked vegetables and blend in a mixer then return to the stock. Heat gently stirring in 125ml of cream and 1 tbsp chopped mint. Season with sea salt and black pepper.

POTATOES
Solanum tuberosum

It is difficult to imagine life without the humble spud. Choose varieties that are high on flavour, with unusual textures and which command high prices in the shops. Aim for early, mid and late varieties to have a constant supply for nine months of the year.

When to Plant
Early spring.

Where to Plant
Purchase seed potatoes in late winter and keep them in a cool, light space in the warm, to sprout green shoots. This process is known as chitting, and gains you several weeks of growth whilst waiting for the earth to warm up. Plant in fertile soil that has been well forked over. Add some well-rotted compost to the surface, but do not use fresh manure. Plant the tubers 15 cm deep and 40 cm apart allowing 45 cm between rows of early varieties and 75 cm for mid and late varieties.

Cultivation
When the first shoots appear, draw the earth from between the rows to cover and protect the green growth from a late frost. This also encourages the growth of underground tubers and thus more potatoes.

Once the flowers appear, soak potato plants once a week in dry weather and feed with a general organic fertilizer along the row once a month. If there is a sudden late frost, the leaves may blacken and wilt. Cut them back and they should re-emerge without affecting the potatoes.

Harvesting & Storing
When the first flower buds appear on the early crop, lift a tuber to check the size of the potatoes. If large enough, dig up as required. This will be about 14 weeks after planting. With main crop and late varieties, wait until the leaves have turned brown about 20 weeks after planting, then carefully dig up the whole crop. Discard any damaged or diseased ones and store in paper sacks in a dry, cool place, free from frost.

Varieties

Early Potatoes

Oria is blight-resistant and has an excellent texture for sautéing.

Belle de Fontenay keeps its shape when cooked so very good for making flavoursome potato salads.

Mid Potatoes

Charlotte has a waxy texture and is good as a mid-season variety.

Nicola has an excellent flavour and firm flesh for salads.

Late Potatoes

Pink Fir Apple is ideal for winter potato salads and will keep until Christmas.

Valor is one of the most disease-resistant potatoes, good for baking or mashing.

Pests & Diseases

Potato eelworm, tomato and potato blight.

Tortilla

Cut 500g new potatoes and 1 medium onion into 2.5 cm cubes. Fry with a crushed clove of garlic in 75g of olive oil for 30–40 minutes on a very low heat until the potatoes are cooked. The onions should be golden not brown to bring out their flavour so keep an eye on the heat. Add 6 beaten eggs, sea salt and black pepper and cook very gently for 5 minutes until the eggs are beginning to set. Place under a hot grill for 5 more minutes. When cool tip out on to a plate and serve with a salad of mixed leaves and lettuce.

■ ■ ■

PUMPKINS
Cucurbita maxima

Pumpkins, unlike squash, can be disappointing as edible plants, but children will enjoy growing them for Halloween lanterns.

When to Plant
Late spring.

Where to Plant
Sow one seed to an 9 cm pot in early spring, keep indoors on a sunny windowsill. They will be ready to plant out 4–6 weeks after sowing provided all frosts are over. Choose a sunny position in fertile soil, spacing bush types 1.5 metres apart and trailing types 2.5 metres apart.

Cultivation
Water once a week if the weather is dry and mulch with garden compost.

Harvesting & Storing
Most pumpkins will be ready for cropping in early autumn, although they can be left a few weeks in the ground to soak up more sun if necessary. Pumpkins do not store well, but should be kept in a warm dry place and used by early winter.

Varieties
Baby Bear has golden orange fruit and is deliciously tasty when baked. Roast the seeds in olive oil for an extra treat.
White Large grows into a dramatic, rich creamy-skinned pumpkin containing red-orange flesh. It's very disease-resistant.

Pests & Diseases
Slugs in the first few weeks.

Pumpkin Soup

In a large saucepan put 500g of pumpkin cut into 2.5 cm cubes, a chopped medium onion and 2 cloves of crushed garlic. Add 25g of butter and 1 tsp of thyme leaves. Cover with a lid and stew very gently for 10 mins. Add 225g of chopped, skinned tomatoes and 1 pint/550 ml of vegetable stock, and simmer until the pumpkin is very tender—about 30 mins. Liquidize and return to the pan to keep warm. The soup should be quite thick. Blend 1 tsp of powdered coriander, paprika, cumin, ¼ tsp of chilli and 2 chopped spring onions in 50g of butter. Pour the piping hot soup into bowls and dollop a teaspoon of spicy butter on to the surface of soup. Serve with hot bread.

RADISHES
Raphanus sativus

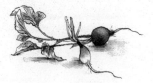

These are probably the easiest vegetables to grow, and the quickest from seed to plate. Summer-sown radishes take twenty to forty days to mature, making them a useful catch crop.

When to Sow
Mid-spring to late summer.

Where to Sow
Radishes like moist, fertile soil. Sow every four weeks directly in the ground, protected by a cloche, from late winter until early spring. From then on and until early summer, sow a little seed every two weeks in open ground. Sow winter radishes from late summer onwards. Sow in shallow drills 1 cm deep in rows 15 cm apart. Thin to 5–7 cm for summer varieties as soon as the seedlings can be handled. Winter radishes can be spaced 10 cm apart and will take sixty to eighty days to mature.

Cultivation
They need little attention, but water once a week in very dry weather.

Harvesting & Storing
Summer varieties should be picked as soon as they are useable. Winter crops are best lifted in mid-winter before damage from frost or slugs. Twist off their tops and store in boxes of sand.

Varieties
French Breakfast has long red roots with a crisp, fleshy texture.
Scarlet Globe is an old variety with a good hot flavour.

Pests & Diseases
Flea beetles.

Radishes with Crusty Bread

Wash 24 radishes, chill in a bowl of iced water for 30 minutes to crisp up, then pat dry on a tea towel. Put 6 on each plate with a ball of best organic butter and a mound of sea salt. Serve with crusty bread.

SPINACH *Spinacea oleracea*
& SWISS CHARD *Beta vulgaris*

True spinach, leaf beet (sometimes called perpetual spinach) and Swiss chard are all members of the beet family. True spinach is an annual and tends to bolt by early summer. Leaf beet (perpetual spinach) is a perennial and easier to grow than true spinach. Swiss chard is the most decorative member of the beet family, available in a huge array of stem colours: yellow, orange, red, pink and green.

When to Sow
Early spring and early autumn.

Where to Sow
True spinach should be sown in short rows in the ground, starting in early spring. Do not sow in summer but sow again early autumn. Sow in any space, even part shade, in moisture-retentive soil. Thin the seedlings to 30 cm apart each way. Crop the leaves when they are still small: about 5 cm to 10 cm for salad or 15 cm to 20 cm for cooking.

Leaf beet (perpetual spinach) tolerates a drier soil, is less likely to run to seed, and can be sown as for true spinach. As soon as the seedlings can be handled, thin initially to 10 cm, composting the surplus seedlings. You will need to thin again, and these more substantial plants can be re-positioned in another row spacing them 30 cm apart each way.

Swiss chard is sown in mid-spring and spaced in the same way as perpetual spinach.

All three plants can be sown in seed trays before being planted out individually.

Cultivation
True spinach should be allowed to grow to 15–20 cm before cropping. It will not re-grow. Leaf beet (perpetual spinach) and Swiss chard will benefit from a top dressing of organic fertilizer to produce more leaves in late summer. Water once a week.

Harvesting & Storing
Pick regularly to encourage leaf production.
Freeze any surplus by cooking and chopping it up prior to freezing.

Varieties

True Spinach

True Spinach has no named varieties so look for a packet of true spinach seeds *(Beta vulgaris)*.

Leaf Beet (Perpetual Spinach)

Spinach Matador has large slightly blistered leaves and is good for a summer harvest.

Giant Winter is a hardy variety and will survive winter if sown in autumn to extend the harvest.

Swiss Chard

Swiss Chard produces fat, pearly-white stems—delicious fried in butter.

Bright Lights has multi-coloured leaves of red, yellow and green that retain their colour on cooking.

Pests & Diseases

Occasionally aphids.

Catalonian Spinach with Pine Kernels and Raisins

Wash 1 kg of spinach, drain and place in a large saucepan with 1 tsp of sea salt. Heat gently and cook until wilted, about 3–5 minutes. Squeeze out excess water, roughly chop and keep hot in a serving dish. Heat 5 tbsps of olive oil in a frying pan and sauté 2 crushed cloves of garlic, 45g of pine nuts and 50g of raisins. Stir fry for 2 minutes then pour the sizzling mixture over the cooked spinach stirring it in. Excellent with lamb or grilled fish.

SQUASH
Cucurbita pepo

There are many varieties of squash, most of which store well, providing you with produce well into the winter and following spring.

When to Plant
Late spring.

Where to Sow
All squash require a sunny, sheltered site in fertile soil. Sow on a sunny windowsill in early spring, two seeds to each 9 cm pot, taking out the weaker one when big enough to handle. Keep well watered. When all threat of frost has passed, dig a hole big enough to take a couple of spades full of well-rotted manure. Fill up with topsoil and plant so that the lowest leaves are level with the ground. Plant when the seedlings are 14 cm tall, spacing them 75 cm apart each way.

Harvesting & Storing
Squash take about four months to mature but can be left in the ground until frosts are forecast. Cut and store in a warm, dry place.

Varieties
Butternut Squash has easy to prepare, bright orange flesh, excellent for roasting.
Futsu is a small, slightly ribbed fruit that stores well into spring.

Pests & Diseases
Slugs and mildew.

Butternut Squash Risotto

Cut a butternut squash into 2.5 cm thick, boat-shaped slices and place on a baking sheet, skin-side down. Add salt and pepper and drizzle with olive oil. Bake for 20 minutes at 200°C. Slice off the skin and cube into bite-size pieces, then add these to a traditional risotto ten minutes before the rice is finished cooking. Serve with freshly grated parmesan and adjust the seasoning.

SWEETCORN
Zea mays

Sweetcorn requires a fairly long, warm season to mature, but is otherwise very easy to grow.

When to Plant
Late spring.

Where to Sow
Choose a sheltered position in full sun, in moisture-retaining, rich soil. Best results are achieved by sowing indoors in mid-spring, sowing two seeds to a 9 cm pot, thinned to one when well established. When all danger of frost is over, plant out 35 cm apart. Sweetcorn relies on the wind to self-pollinate, and to assist this, grow in blocks of four rather than in straight rows.

Cultivation
Weed regularly but take care—the roots of sweetcorn are very near the surface so avoid damaging plants with the hoe. They need lots of water, so mulch the base of each plant with well-rotted garden compost or farmyard manure to help conserve moisture.

Harvesting & Storing
From planting to harvest takes 12–16 weeks, and the cobs are ready when the silk tassels turn dark brown. Cut the cob from the main branch with a sharp knife. Cook within three days of picking or freeze.

Varieties
Double Standard produces very large, fleshy cobs in late summer.
Golden Bantam An old favourite with a very sweet flavour, cropping from mid-late summer.
It is best not to mix different varieties in any one year, since cross-pollination may occur which will result in tough starchy kernels.

Pests & Diseases
Mice and slugs can damage seed sown directly in the ground.

Sweetcorn with Coriander Butter

Mash some butter, black pepper and chopped coriander leaves in a bowl. Boil the sweetcorn for about 15 minutes and spread the coriander butter over the sweetcorn to serve.

■ ■ ■

TOMATOES *Lycopersicon esculentum*

Tomatoes can be time-consuming to grow on the allotment, needing daily watering when the fruit has set, a twice-weekly feed and regular tying in to get the best results. Try bush varieties, as they are easier to grow and stop at a pre-determined height.

When to Plant
Late spring.

Where to Sow
The most successful way to grow tomatoes is to sow seed in pots every two weeks from mid-spring. Place two seeds in a 9 cm pot and keep watered on a sunny windowsill. Remove the weaker of the two seedlings when the leaves are fully expanded. A week before planting out in early summer, harden off during the day in a cold frame. The best time to plant in the ground is when the flowers on the bottom truss are beginning to show colour.

Tomatoes are susceptible to potato blight, so should be grown as far as possible from potatoes in the most sheltered, sunny site on the plot. Space them 45 cm apart with 60 cm between rows in well-drained rich, moisture-retentive soil. The largest size Gro-bag will take four bush tomatoes. They will produce fruit over a period of four weeks about sixteen weeks after planting, so plant sequentially to crop throughout the summer.

Cultivation
Bush tomatoes will need staking to keep the fruit off the ground, so tie them to canes as they grow. Feed with organic tomato feed every ten days.

Harvesting & Storing

Pick the tomatoes regularly, and if you have a glut, cook them into soups or sauces for the freezer. Frost damages the fruit, so pick unripe ones to make into a green tomato salsa or chutney.

Varieties

Ace 55 is a bush variety producing long red fruit that keep well on the plant without splitting.

Gardener's Delight is an old variety that produces a high yield of sweet, tasty, little fruit.

Pests & Diseases

Aphids, spider mite, tomato blight.

Tomato Sauce

To make 475ml of sauce, melt 25g of butter with 2 tbsps of olive oil. Add 1–4 crushed garlic cloves and cook for 2 minutes until golden brown. Add a finely sliced medium onion and cook for a further 2 minutes before adding 900g of peeled and chopped tomatoes. Season with sea salt, black pepper and 1 tsp of sugar. Cook fast for 15–20 minutes then purée and adjust the seasoning. Freeze to store.

Fruit

Soft fruit requires a permanent bed and quite a lot of attention to be successful. However, most of the work can be done in the autumn when there is less to do elsewhere in your plot.

I have not included details of fruit trees, but if you want to grow them choose dwarf stock to avoid shading neighbouring plots. Look in a garden centre or in seed catalogues to see what small fruit trees are available. Apples, damsons, plums and pears have all been developed on a dwarf rootstock and can be grown as bush or cordon crops. A cordon is restricted to a single stem 1.5 metres to 2 metres long, clothed with fruiting spears to produce a high yield in a small area.

BLACKBERRIES
Rubus fruticosus

The scent of cooked blackberries is one of the best consolations for the end of summer.

When to Plant
Mid-winter.

Where to Plant
Site in deep, well prepared soil, in sun or part shade. Blackberries are greedy feeders, so dig in lots of organic matter before planting.

Buy one-year-old plants in containers, planting them 3 metres apart with 2 metres between rows.

Cultivation
In spring be ready with a support system as for raspberries, tying plants in as they grow. After fruiting, cut down the old canes to ground level and tie in the new canes as they emerge.

Harvesting & Storing
Pick the berries on a dry day when the fruit are black but before they get too soft. A surplus can be cooked and frozen.

Varieties
Ashton Cross has a flavour closest to wild blackberries.
Oregon Thornless produces masses of delicious berries and is easy to harvest.

Pests & Diseases
Raspberry beetle, downy mildew.

Blackberry and Apple Crumble

One of the best autumn puddings! Stew 350g of Bramley apples with 30g of sugar in 1 tbsp of water. When they are half-cooked, stir in 150g of blackberries and tip into a pie dish. Rub 50g each of butter into 110g plain flour, add 50g caster sugar and sprinkle over the fruit. Cook for 30–45 minutes at 180°C. Serve with clotted cream.

CURRANTS
Ribes nigrum

Freshly picked currants are intensely perfumed and transform the simplest of desserts.

When to Plant
Late autumn to mid-winter.

Where to Plant
Mature redcurrant and blackcurrant bushes can spread to 1.8 metres, so bear this in mind when planning your fruit beds. Buy two-year-old container-grown bushes from certified stock. Space them every 150 cm in rows 180 cm apart. All currants will tolerate some shade, but the fruit will taste better if grown in full sun. Blackcurrants should be planted

about 2 cm deeper than they were in the pot—you can use the soil mark on the plant to guide you. This will encourage more shoots to grow from below the ground thus increasing the crop. Redcurrants should be planted at the same depth as they were in the pot, since they produce fruit on a stem from the main branch.

Cultivation

Prune black- and redcurrants in summer by taking out the stems that carried the fruit. The one-year-old stems that have pushed through from the ground will produce next year's crop. Protect with netting against birds in spring. Water in dry weather but not as the fruit ripens, this might cause the skins to split. Both these fruits benefit from a dressing of potash around their roots in late winter: 15g per square metre.

Harvesting & Storing

Pick red- and blackcurrants in complete clusters, not individually, when they feel fat and firm. Bottle, preserve or freeze.

Varieties

Blackcurrants

Ben Connan has very large berries with an exceptional flavour.
Ben Tirran crops later and is frost-resistant, making it useful to extend the season.

Redcurrants

Rovada is a very heavy cropper with an excellent flavour.
Junifer produces juicy, sharp redcurrants early in the summer.

Pests & Diseases

Aphids, blackcurrant gall mite, and birds.

Blackcurrant Sorbet

Purée 450g of freshly picked blackcurrants in a liquidizer. Rub through a sieve and add 200g of caster sugar. Freeze immediately in a shallow bowl (the sugar will dissolve). Whisk it once or twice over the next 5 hours to break up the ice crystals. Decorate with bunches of redcurrants dipped in iced water and then caster sugar.

GOOSEBERRIES
Ribes grossularia

Gooseberries are one of the earliest fruits to crop. They are high in pectin, so make an ideal fruit for jam.

When to Plant
Autumn.

Where to Plant
Space the bushes 1.5 metres apart in moist, rich soil. Gooseberries will tolerate some shade. Add well-rotted manure in the planting hole. Two-year-old plants will guarantee fruit the following year.

Cultivation
Net the fruit in early spring to protect against birds, and keep watered to avoid the fruit splitting. Mulch with well-rotted manure each spring. Protect with a mesh or net against birds. Prune in winter by removing one in three of the thickest branches.

Harvesting & Storing
Pick the berries when they are still firm, usually late spring. Gooseberries freeze well.

Varieties
Rokula has juicy red fruit that retain their colour when cooked. It is mildew-resistant.
Leveller produces extra large fruit, with an excellent flavour.

Pests & Diseases
Downy mildew, grey mould, birds.

Gooseberry and Mint Jelly

Wash 1 kg of ripe gooseberries, no need to top or tail them. Put in a pan with 250ml of water and simmer gently until the fruit is soft and broken. Sieve the fruit, pushing with a metal spoon to get as much flesh as possible. To each pint of juice add 300g of sugar, 1 tbsp of wine vinegar and 4 tbsps of finely chopped fresh mint. Boil until the jelly sets when dropped on a plate. Delicious with roast lamb.

RASPBERRIES
Rubus idaeus

Raspberries produce summer or autumn fruit so are excellent for extending the soft fruit season.

When to Plant
Autumn.

Where to Plant
Raspberries need a sheltered sunny or part-shaded site with well-drained soil. Clear the ground of all weeds and add lots of well-rotted manure. Purchase disease-free certified canes and space them 50 cm apart, leaving 1 metre between rows for picking. Consider one row of summer and one row of autumn fruiting varieties if space allows.

Cultivation
In early spring support the plants' rapid growth with posts and wire. Bang in posts 5 cm square, 2 metres high at each end of the row, and secure three lengths of gardening wire horizontally between them at 50 cm intervals. Tie in the new growth to these wires—they will grow fast and reach the top by summer.

Pick the fruit and cut the cane that has fruited down to the ground after picking. Mulch generously each spring to keep the weeds down and help retain moisture. Autumn varieties can be cut down to the ground in spring, as new growth begins. Water plants regularly and thoroughly.

Harvesting & Storing
Pick the fruit on a dry day, pulling the berries off and leaving the core on the plant. Raspberries freeze well.

Varieties
Glen Moy is fat and juicy and ripens in early summer. It is virus-resistant. **Autumn Bliss** is a delicious late variety. In a sheltered position it will fruit till early winter.

Pests & Diseases
Raspberry beetle, grey mould.

Raspberry Pavlova

Pre-heat the oven to 150°C. Whip 2 egg whites until you can turn the bowl upside down and they stay put. Fold in 110g of caster sugar a tablespoon at a time. Spread in a round on oiled silicone paper, on a baking tray. Place in the oven and immediately reduce temperature to 140°C. Cook for 1 hour then leave to cool. Spread with 225g of whipped cream and 225g of raspberries.

■ ■ ■

RHUBARB
Rheum rhabarbarum

Rhubarb produces the first fruit of the season and can be forced as early as late winter.

When to Plant
Spring to autumn.

Where to Plant
Buy crowns (fleshy rootstock with one bud) and set them 1.2 metres apart in well-drained soil in sun or part shade. Before planting dig in plenty of manure or compost—rhubarb is a hungry feeder.

Cultivation
Water the base of the plant in dry weather. Cut back dead foliage in autumn and mulch with well-rotted manure. Traditional terracotta forcing pots or a bucket at least 45 cm high, placed over the plant in late winter, encourages the emerging shoots to grow tall and tender as they seek the light. The leaves contain oxalic acid and are toxic, but you would have to eat about 5 kg to get a fatal dose. If there is a severe frost in early spring the leaves may leak acid into the stems, and these should not be eaten. Both leaves and stem will do no harm in the compost heap.

Harvesting & Storing
Select the stems that have fully unfolded leaves, as these will be ready for eating. Stop harvesting after three months so that the plant can build up strength to produce good stems for next year.

Varieties

Cawood Delight produces tender and delicious stems over a long period.

Hawke's Champayne is an early variety with a fabulous, refreshing flavour.

Pests & Diseases

Rhubarb is generally free of trouble. If the crown rots, lift and replace either by dividing another plant or purchasing a healthy new crown.

Rhubarb Jam

To make 1.5 kg of jam: put 900g of rhubarb, thickly sliced, and 900g of granulated sugar into a pan. Stir over a medium heat until the sugar has dissolved. Add the juice of one lemon and boil for about 15 minutes. Skim off any scum, test for setting and allow to cool before ladling into clean hot jars. Store for at least one month before eating.

■ ■ ■

STRAWBERRIES
Fragaria x ananassa

Strawberries, being herbaceous perennials, will die back in winter to re-emerge the following spring.

When to Plant

Late summer to early autumn.

Where to Plant

Purchase plants from certified stock and plant in fresh ground that has not had strawberries in it for at least three years. The soil must be weed-free and prepared with garden compost or manure. Place the plants firmly in the ground, with the base of the crown at soil level. Space 45 cm apart with 75 cm between rows and water well. Growing strawberries through straw will help to retain moisture, keep weeds down, and protect the fruit from soil splash.

Cultivation

Keep the ground weed-free and water regularly. Plants should be renewed every three years and can be propagated from the runners that are put out from the main plant each year. To renew, select the youngest plants and sever them from the parent, which you should discard. Reposition the young runner in fresh ground, since cropping, fruit size and health deteriorate if the same ground is used.

Harvesting & Storing

Harvest as soon as the fruit is red. Surplus can be made into jam or puréed and frozen. After harvesting it is best to cut off all foliage and flower stalks, and sever and pull up any runners. You will only need the new runners every three years when you are renewing your plants.

Varieties

Royal Sovereign is an old traditional variety with a superb flavour. *Cambridge Favourite* is the perfect choice for jam-making.

Pests & Diseases

Grey mould in wet summers, slugs and birds.

Strawberry Yoghurt Icecream

Purée 900g of ripe strawberries in a blender. Heat 175ml of grape juice in a pan until boiling. Remove from the heat and stir in 1 tsp of powdered gelatine until dissolved. Pour onto 2 beaten egg yolks and fold in 250ml of Greek yoghurt and the strawberry purée. Freeze until crystals form round the edges. Whisk the egg whites until stiff and fold into the half-frozen icecream. Freeze until solid.

Herbs

If you use lots of herbs, then make a good size bed in a sheltered, sunny spot. Parsley, chives, basil and fennel help to repel aphids, and many other herbs scent the air encouraging bees and butterflies. You can't have too many in my view—they transform the simplest of ingredients. Pick a mixed bunch every time you visit the allotment.

To make the bed, prepare the ground in the usual way, adding compost to give the herbs a good start. Most like well-drained, sunny conditions with a feed in spring. If you are planting in very hot weather, you will need to water frequently until the plant is established.

Many herbs are perennials so will return each year and all benefit from regular picking to keep them in shape. Shrubby perennial herbs grown from seed will take 12–18 months to mature, so buy these as established plants. Look for sturdy, bushy plants and group them together, spacing them as instructed on the pot. Do not be tempted to buy pots of herbs from the supermarket, as these are grown to last only a few weeks.

Annual herbs can be sown from seed to keep costs down. To dry herbs pick them on a sunny day, hang them up in a warm dry space for a week or so, then pull the leaves off the stems and store in airtight containers. Many herbs freeze well. Wash small quantities, shake them dry and put in tiny bags. Label carefully, as herbs look very similar when frozen!

BASIL
Ocimum basilicum

There are several exciting varieties of basil to experiment with: try cinnamon, Thai and lemon scented leaves, or the purple-leaved ones which look very dramatic shredded over red pepper and tomato salads.

When to Plant
Early summer.

Where to Sow
Basil is an annual, so you can experiment with different varieties each year. Sow in a seed tray on a sunny windowsill in early spring. Thin the seedlings out one to each 9 cm pot, and keep behind glass. Basil is frost-tender, so wait until early summer to put in the ground. Space the plants 20 cms apart.

Cultivation
Be vigilant for slug attack and keep well watered. Give a liquid feed every four weeks.

Harvesting & Storing
Harvest the leaves from the top of the plant to encourage bushy growth; any surplus can be made into pesto.

Varieties
Genovese Basil is the classic Italian herb with a very sweet flavour.
Basil Lime has small, citrus-flavoured leaves and is delicious added to fish dishes.

Tips for Use
Basil is an essential ingredient in Italian cooking and the foundation for pesto sauce.

You can preserve whole sprigs of basil in olive oil for months. Use the leaves as needed, and the oil can be used to cook Mediterranean dishes.

■　■　■

BAY
Laurus nobilis

The evergreen scented leaves are an essential part of bouquet garni, and no serious cook should be without them.

When to Plant
Spring through to autumn.

Where to Plant
Bay is a perennial and slow to grow from seed. Buy a decent-size plant and position for maximum protection from cold winds and severe frosts.

Cultivation
Keep it to a manageable size by regularly picking the leaves and cutting back the branches by a third in spring.

Harvesting & Storing
Pick and store the leaves in a jar in small quantities; newly dried bay has the best flavour.

Tips for Use
Add 2 fresh or dried leaves to rice pudding prior to cooking. The subtle flavour will permeate the creamy rice and each bowl can be further enhanced with a dollop of home-made strawberry jam.

CHIVES
Allium schoenoprasum

This herb is part of the onion family and a good aphid repellant. The tufts of grassy foliage and mauve flower heads are both edible.

When to Sow
Late spring or early autumn.

Where to Sow
Chives are perennial and easy to grow from seed. Sow in drills directly in the ground 1.5 cm deep. Thin or transplant to 15 cm apart.

Cultivation
Established clumps can be lifted and divided every three years.

Harvesting & Storing
Chives are best eaten fresh, but they do freeze well. Snip them from frozen with scissors.

Varieties
Garlic or **Oriental Chives** (*Allium tuberosum*) are delicious added to stir fry.

Tips for Use
Pick the flower heads and inspect for bugs, but try to avoid washing them. Pull out the petals to scatter over salads after you have tossed the salad leaves in dressing.

■ ■ ■

CORIANDER
Coriandrum sativum

Coriander is an annual—a delicious herb essential for Indian and Middle Eastern cooking. It is easy to grow and tolerant of part shade.

When to Sow
Mid-spring.

Where to Sow
Sow in drills directly in the ground 0.5 cm deep, and thin to 10 cm between plants.

Cultivation
Coriander quickly runs to seed so sow fortnightly, in short rows. Be vigilant for slugs and water in dry weather.

Harvesting & Storing
Use fresh, as coriander does not freeze well, or store in oil as for basil.

Varieties
Coriander Chechnya produces a good leafy crop.
Coriander Slobolt is slow to go to seed.

Tips for Use
If your coriander runs to seed you can rub the seeds off and store in a dry jar. Crush with a pestle and mortar and use in Indian cooking or add whole to chutneys and pickles.

DILL
Anethum graveolens

Dill is an annual and one of the prettiest of the flowering herbs. It is an essential ingredient for fish dishes.

When to Sow
Spring to early summer.

Where to Sow
Sow as for chives and thin to 15 cm with 30 cm between plants.

Cultivation
Water well in dry spells, and pick leaves regularly before the plant flowers.

Harvesting & Storing
Dill is best eaten fresh—it does not freeze well. Dill seeds can be stored in a dry jar to add to pickles.

Varieties
Dill Tetra produces an abundance of blue-green leaves that set off the deep yellow flowers.

Mammoth may run to seed rather fast but will provide a useful store of fragrant seeds for cooking.

Tips for Use
Dill is traditionally used in fish dishes. It is also delicious chopped up in scrambled eggs and potato salad.

■ ■ ■

FENNEL
Foeniculum vulgare

Fennel fronds are similar to dill but have a distinct, sweet aniseed flavour.

When to Sow
Spring.

Where to Sow
Fennel is a perennial and can be sown from seed as for chives, in drills 6 mm deep; thin to 30 cm apart. Alternatively buy container-grown plants and dig in the ground.

Cultivation
It will die back in winter to-emerge in spring. After three years divide the clumps as for chives, and re-plant.

Harvesting & Storing
Pick the fresh fronds for use in salads or cooking. Fennel does not freeze well. The seeds can be kept in a dry container and added to pickles or crushed and used in Indian cooking.

Varieties
Bronze Fennel is very decorative, with strong bronze foliage.

Tips for Use
Add chopped fennel leaves to new potatoes dressed with sour cream. This is excellent as a summer salad to accompany barbecued fish.

■ ▓ ■

HYSSOP
Hyssopus officinalis

Hyssop helps to lure the cabbage butterfly from the brassica bed. The leaf has a delicate scent and is good with tomato salads.

When to Sow
Spring to autumn.

Where to Sow
Hyssop is a perennial and slow to grow from seed. Look for good size plants in 2 litre pots and space 30 cm apart.

Cultivation
Pick regularly to keep the bush in shape.

Harvesting & Storing
The leaves are evergreen and can be dried or frozen.

Tips for Use
Add a sprig or two to the syrup used for stewing dried apricots or prunes.

■ ■ ■

LEMON BALM
Melissa officinalis

The fresh green leaves of lemon balm are a welcome reminder that spring is on the way. The colour of the leaves somehow reflects the intense lemon scent of this aromatic herb.

When to Plant
Spring to autumn.

Where to Plant
It is slow to grow from seed, so purchase a 9 cm pot plant.

Cultivation
Lemon balm dies back in winter to re-emerge next spring. It will quickly develop into a substantial bush, so divide up and re-plant a small root every three years. It can be invasive, spreading by airborne seeds in summer. To avoid it invading neighbouring plots, cut it back hard before flowering in summer.

Harvesting & Storing
Pick when the leaves are young and fresh in early spring to early summer. It freezes well.

Varieties
Lemon Balm is the only named variety.

Tips for Use
Add to finely chopped onions, breadcrumbs and butter and use as a stuffing for chicken; or add six leaves to a cup of hot water for a refreshing infusion.

LOVAGE
Levisticum officinale

Lovage tastes something like celery with a spicy hint of lemon.

When to Plant
Spring to autumn.

Where to Plant
As a perennial it is slow to grow from seed, so buy a container-grown plant. Lovage grows to 1.5 metres, and one plant gives lots of pickings.

Cultivation
It dies back in winter to re-emerge in spring. Be vigilant for slugs as new shoots emerge in spring.

Harvesting & Storing
Pick the leaves when they are young and add to stocks or soup. The leaves dry easily for winter use. If it forms a flower, dry the seeds and store in a jar.

Varieties
Lovage is the only named variety.

Tips for Use
Stem, leaf and seeds can all be used in soups or sauces. Finely chopped lovage makes a delicious alternative to mint on broad beans.

■ ■ ■

MARJORAM
Origanum vulgare

Marjoram combines brilliantly with tomato and cheese for simple vegetarian dishes.

When to Plant
Late spring.

Where to Plant
As a tender perennial it is difficult to grow from seed, so buy a couple of 9 cm pots and plant them 20 cm apart.

Cultivation
Marjoram dies back in winter to re-emerge in spring. It is susceptible to frosts, so cover with a cloche or straw on winter.

Harvesting & Storing
Pick the leaves and dry before storing in an airtight jar.

Varieties
Pot marjoram *(Origanum onites)* produces an abundance of purply-pink flowers, attracting bees for the whole of the summer. It has a delicate, mild flavour and is good in tomato salads.
Sweet marjoram *(Origanum majorana)* has a stronger, sweeter flavour, excellent for adding to marinades.

Tips for Use
Add chopped marjoram when possible towards the end of cooking to maximize the flavour.

■　■　■

PARSLEY
Petroselinum crispum

This is the curly-leafed variety, traditionally used in parsley sauce. All parsley is tolerant of shade.

When to Sow
Mid-spring and early autumn.

Where to Sow
Parsley is a biennial, but the leaves become coarse in their second year so treat as an annual. Sow as for coriander but be prepared for a six-week germination period.

Cultivation
Pick regularly and if a flower head appears, leave it to self-seed.

Harvesting & Storing
Pick the leaves and stem to use fresh, as it loses flavour when dried. Parsley freezes well.

Varieties
French parsley *(Petroselinum var. neapolitanum)* has a flat leaf and a strong flavour. It is an essential ingredient in Middle Eastern dishes.

Tips for Use
Parsley is highly favoured by herbalists for its diuretic and anti-rheumatic properties. Chop it finely and mix with butter and garlic to flavour grilled meat and fish.

■ ■ ■

PEPPERMINT
Mentha piperita

This is the mint used for infusions and is an excellent natural digestive—the one herb never to be without! It is an essential sauce for roast lamb, and adds beauty and flavour to many simple Middle Eastern recipes.

When to Plant
Spring.

Where to Plant
As a perennial it is difficult to grow from seed, so buy one or two plants in 9 cm pots. Mint is notorious for running underground and invading other beds, so contain the roots. Dig a hole big enough to take a bucket, fill with soil and plant. The roots will have enough nutrients and water but no opportunity to rampage around the plot.

Cultivation
Pick the leaves regularly to encourage bushy plants. In autumn, lift the plant and divide, re-planting one half. It will die back to re-emerge next spring. Alternatively plant several 10 cm long pieces with their roots in a 30 cm pot. Keep watered on a sunny windowsill, conservatory or porch for a winter supply of fresh mint.

Harvesting & Storing
Pick as required. Mint dries and freezes well.

Varieties
Spearmint *(Mentha spicatais)* is the culinary mint which can be added chopped to beans and potatoes.
Apple mint *(Mentha suavelens)* has round woolly leaves and a slight apple smell.
Bowles mint *(Mentha rotundifolia)* is considered best for mint sauce. Grow all of these as for peppermint.

Tips for Use
Add 1 tbsp of finely chopped spearmint to a bowl of crab apple jelly to serve with roast lamb.

■　■　■

ROSEMARY
Rosemarinus officinalis

Rosemary is often in flower in late winter, making it a great bee attractant for early pollination.

When to Sow
Spring to autumn.

Where to Sow
Rosemary is a perennial and slow to grow from seed. Look for good size plants in 2 litre pots and space 30 cm apart.

Cultivation
Pick regularly to keep the bush in shape.

Harvesting & Storing
The leaves are evergreen and can be dried or frozen.

Varieties
Miss Jessop's Upright grows tall and bushy.

Tips for Use
Pull the leaves off rosemary and add towards the end of roasting vegetables. It can also be used in sweet dishes: grind rosemary flowers with sugar and use to flavour creams and custard.

SAGE
Salvia officinalis

Pineapple-scented, purple and golden-leafed varieties are all edible, and the summer flowers are another great bee attractant.

When to Sow
Spring to autumn.

Where to Sow
Sage is a perennial and can be sown from seed directly in the ground late spring for strong plants the following autumn. Sow in drills 1 cm deep and thin to final planting distance 45 cm. Alternatively buy plants in 9 cm pots and space accordingly.

Cultivation
Sage produces fewer leaves as it gets older so will need replacing every three to four years.

Propagate by pinning the side shoots (bare except for a few green leaves at the top) into the ground. These will root in about eight weeks and can then be cut from the main plant and repositioned, spacing as above.

Harvesting & Storing
Pick the leaves fresh as you need them. Sage freezes well.

Varieties
Golden Sage (*Salvia officinalis var. Icterina*) has variegated gold-green leaves that look pretty torn up and sprinkled over tomato salads.
Pineapple Sage (*Salvia elegans*) has a distinct pineapple flavour and cut finely can be added to fruit salads. It is frost-tender, so take cuttings and pot up to keep on a sunny windowsill over the winter.

Tips for Use
Use sage sparingly, it has a very strong flavour even after cooking. For this reason it is excellent with fatty meats such as pork or duck.

SUMMER SAVORY
Satureja hortensis

Savory combines all the scents of thyme, sage and marjoram. It is another good bee attractant, and a good companion plant for beans to assist pollination.

When to Plant
Mid-spring.

Where to Plant
As a perennial it is slow to grow from seed, so buy plants in 9 cm pots and space them 45 cm apart.

Cultivation
Keep the plant in shape by regular picking. It loses flavour if it produces flowers.

Harvesting & Storing
Use the leaves fresh in summer and dry them for winter use.

Varieties
Winter Savory (*Satureja Montana*) is an annual with a stronger, less sweet flavour than the summer variety. It is tolerant of baking hot conditions and can be sown from seed (follow the instructions for Basil).

Tips for Use
Savory is one of few herbs that has a better flavour when used dried. It combines brilliantly with dried bean soups and pasta dishes, both of which soak up the scents.

TARRAGON
Artemesia dracunculus sativa

This is the French tarragon, and it has a more intense aniseed flavour than the Russian one.

When to Sow
Spring.

Where to Sow
As a perennial it is slow to grow from seed. Buy two or three plants in 9 cm pots spacing them 30 cm apart to give a good clump. It takes a couple of years to form a sizeable plant.

Cultivation
Protect from severe frost in winter with a cloche or fleece.

Harvesting & Storing
Pinch out the top third of the stems for cooking and to promote a bushy plant. The flavour is strongest in summer. Tarragon freezes well.

Tips for Use
Cut a long sprig of tarragon and immerse in a bottle of white wine vinegar. Use for salad dressings, especially those served with cold roast chicken dishes.

■ ■ ■

THYME
Thymus vulgaris

There are hundreds of varieties of thyme, including orange, lemon and caraway-scented leaves. The flowers are edible and a good bee attractant.

When to Sow
Spring to autumn.

Where to Sow
These short-lived perennials are slow to grow from seed, so buy several 9 cm pots and plant them 30 cm apart.

Cultivation
Trim plants after flowering to keep them in shape.

Harvesting & Storing
Pick the woody stems as needed, pulling the leaves off. Dry whole branches for winter use.

Varieties
Lemon Thyme (*Thymus citriodorus*) is a blend of sharp lemon and warm thyme.
Broad-Leaved Thyme (*Thymus pulegoides*) has large fleshy leaves that give an intense flavour to roasts.

Tips for Use
Lemon thyme enhances the flavour of farmed fish, which is sometimes rather bland. A sprig tucked in to the cavity of salmon or trout before grilling gives a delicious lemony scent.

Flowers

Make room in any of your four plots for a row or two of flowers. As well as flowers traditionally grown as companion plants, other annuals are included here because they have a long flowering period and are brilliant as cut flowers for the house. With the space on an allotment you can afford to experiment with a row or two of daring, cut flower combinations. Look in the many books on modern flower decoration and in good florist shops for inspiration, then while away the winter evenings planning your cut flower rows.

Sowing seeds is the cheapest method and is a great opportunity to involve children on the allotment.

Prepare the ground by removing stones, weeds or old roots. Fork over and rake flat, breaking up any clods of earth with the back of the rake. Broadcast seed or plant seedlings as instructed; flowers do best if not overcrowded and will generally remain pest-free.

You can even experiment with flamboyant tulips, stately gladioli, and fragrant lilies planted as bulbs in autumn. Stagger the planting over three weeks and pick the flowers in bud. When they are over, lift out the spent bulbs and fill the bare ground with annual flower seeds in early summer. If you want to re-plant the bulbs the following autumn, leave them to die back, then lift and store in a dry shed in paper bags.

■ ■ ■

CALIFORNIAN POPPY
Eschscholzia californica

A good aphid repellant with feathery bluish-green leaves surrounding cup-shaped orange flowers on wiry stems.

When to Sow
Early summer.

Where to Sow
Sow directly in the ground, thinning to 20 cm each way.

Cultivation
Keep the ground weed-free and water in dry weather.

Varieties
Eschscholzia caespitose produces yellow flowers.

■ ■ ■

COSMOS
Cosmos bipinnatus

These flower for weeks on end and the large open flowers attract bees. They vary in colour from purest white through to carmine pink. Their long, sturdy stems make an excellent cut flower in large displays.

When to Sow
Early summer.

Where to Sow
Sow directly in the ground, thinning to 45 cm each way.

Cultivation
Keep the ground weed-free and water in dry weather.

Varieties
Purity has white flowers shown off against soft, apple green leaves.
Sensation produces a mixture of pink, purple and white flowers through till autumn.

FRENCH MARIGOLD
Tagetes patula

French marigold helps repel soil nematodes and whitefly from tomatoes.

Where to Sow
Sow directly in the ground in drills and thin accordingly as they come through, spacing 25–30 cm between plants, or sow seeds in a tray in mid-spring on a sunny windowsill. Harden off outside in the day then plant out early summer.

Cultivation
Keep the ground weed-free and water in dry weather.

Harvesting & Storing
Pick the flowers early in the day. Check for aphids, but try to avoid washing the petals. Add to salads after you have mixed in the salad dressing.

Varieties
Naughty Marietta produces bright orange heads.

■　■　■

LOVE IN A MIST
Nigella damascena

Both flowers and seed heads are excellent as cut flowers. Sowing them near or even in with carrot seeds is believed to keep the crop free of carrot fly.

When to Sow
Mid-spring or late summer.

Where to Sow
Sow directly in the ground thinning to 30 cm each way. Late summer sowing will flower the following year.

Cultivation
Keep the ground weed-free and water in dry weather.

Varieties
Nigella hispanica has deep-blue flowers with crimson crowns in the middle of the flower. It looks wonderful in a pot with dill or fennel flowerheads.
Nigella damascena White has a mid-green ferny leaf that delicately sets off the chalky-white flowers.

■ ■ ■

MORNING GLORY (Dwarf)
Ipomoea tricolor

The dwarf Morning Glory plant is a bushy annual traditionally used as a companion plant to attract hoverflies. The lovely mid-green leaves set off bright, royal blue, trumpet-shaped flowers.

When to Sow
Early spring.

Where to Sow
Sow directly in the ground, thinning to 20 cm each way.

Cultivation
Keep the ground weed-free and water in dry weather.

Varieties
Ensign Series Mixed has a range of four colours.
Heavenly Blue is one of the climbing varieties of Morning Glory.

NASTURTIUM
Nasturtium tropaeolum

These are traditionally grown to attract blackfly away from beans. In order not to lose the nasturtium to the blackfly, a row of marigolds should be planted along side to attract hoverflies to devour the aphids.

When to Sow
Mid-spring.

Where to Sow
Sow directly in the ground, pushing one seed in every 16 cm. The seeds are easy for children to handle and come through fast, visibly growing within two weeks.

Cultivation
Keep the ground weed-free, and water in dry weather. The flowers and small leaves are edible, but check the plant carefully before adding to salad.

Varieties
Empress of India is an old variety that produces opulent ruby-red flowers. *Alaska* has dramatic cream and green variegated leaves setting off large orange flowers.

■ ■ ■

POACHED EGG PLANT
Limnanthes douglasii

The ground-hugging yellow and white flowers are slightly scented and attract hoverflies.

When to Sow
Late spring.

Where to Sow
Sow directly in the ground in drills and thin accordingly as they come through, spacing 15–20 cm between plants. Sow on the edge of the bed. The final height of the plant is 15 cm.

Cultivation
Keep the ground weed-free and water in dry weather. They may well self-seed the following year.

Varieties
No named varieties.

POPPY
Papaver somniferum

This is the bee-attracting opium poppy. The massive tissue paper flowers are followed by lovely silver-green seedpods that are attractive in mixed bunches.

When to Sow
Late spring.

Where to Sow
Sow directly in the ground, thinning to 30 cm each way.

Cultivation
Keep the ground weed-free and water in dry weather.

Varieties
Mrs Perry has huge salmon-pink flowers.
Black Peony has fully double, dark crimson-black flowers.

POT MARIGOLD
Calendula officinalis

Marigolds are key companion plants, grown to attract bees, butterflies, and hoverflies to the allotment.

When to Sow
Early summer.

Where to Sow
Sow directly in the ground in drills and thin accordingly as they come through, spacing 25–30 cm between plants; or sow seeds in a tray in mid-spring on a sunny windowsill. Harden off outside in the day, then plant out early summer.

Cultivation
Keep the ground weed-free and water in dry weather.

Harvesting & Storing
Pick the flowers early in the day, and use in the same way as French marigolds.

Varieties
Indian Prince is a good deep orange.
Spanish Brocade has sturdy stems and is quick to grow, producing a mix of red and gold petals.

SNAPDRAGON
Antirrhinum

This pretty flower is fashionable as a cut flower and valued as much for its form as its lasting qualities in water. It's a great favourite with children and easy to grow. It also attracts bees.

When to Sow
Early summer.

Where to Sow
Sow directly in the ground, thinning to 20 cm each way.

Cultivation
Keep the ground weed-free, protect from slugs and water in dry weather.

Varieties
His Excellency has stunning scarlet flowers that bunch brilliantly with orange and purple flower heads.
F1 White has velvety-white flowers to combine in an all-white display.

■ ■ ■

SUNFLOWER
Helianthus

Children will enjoy sowing and watching these grow to gigantic heights. They are also a rich source of food for birds in autumn.

When to Sow
Early summer.

Where to Sow
Sow directly in the ground, thinning to 30 cm each way.

Cultivation
Keep the ground weed-free, protect from slugs and water in dry weather.

Varieties
Monarch is the giant-headed sunflower that can grow up to 4 metres. **Velvet Queen** produces smaller heads in rich, velvety tones of burgundy, chestnut and bronze. Excellent for bunching with Californian poppies.

■ ■ ■

SWEET PEA
Lathyrus odoratus

Older varieties have the most scent, but all sweet peas are worth growing.

When to Plant
Late spring.

Where to Sow
Sow behind glass in early spring in 9 cm pots and thin to leave four plants to each pot. Pinch out the tips when 3 or 4 pairs of leaves are visible, to bulk out the plant. Plant in the ground about 20 cm apart both ways. Sweet peas can be planted in rows or on wigwams with pea sticks or canes for support; or buy a pot of sweet pea seedlings and show children how to plant two each at the base of four 2-metre bamboo poles, tied into a wigwam. Follow each visit by more watering and tying in, and then have fun picking. A combination of seedlings works best (pots of sweet pea seedlings are inexpensive).

Cultivation
Apply an organic liquid feed every two weeks from mid-summer onwards. Children can pick the lower stems and will see that the more you pick, the more flowers are produced. Water well in dry weather.

Varieties
Painted Lady has delicate pink and white flowers.
Black Knight has deep maroon flowers.
Both of these are old varieties.

Chapter 12

Troubleshooting

The most important aspect of growing healthy produce is to maintain fertile soil with an adequate nutrient content. If the roots have all that they need, so usually will the emerging plant, making it strong enough to withstand and repel attack. Ask your allotment neighbours for advice; people love sharing their experience. Organic gardening focuses on prevention rather than cure, so keep one step ahead with the following tips:

- Buy resistant strains of seeds and seedling vegetables where possible from reliable suppliers.
- Keep your allotment free from chemicals and you will build up a natural population of beneficial insects and predators.

Use companion planting to help reduce pests:

- **French marigolds and Californian poppies** attract hoverflies and ladybirds, which in turn will devour greenfly and aphids. Sow rows of nasturtiums to attract greenfly and blackfly away from young shoots.
- Plant **hyssop** to attract the cabbage butterfly and lure it away from the cabbage.
- **Dill** attracts hoverflies who in turn eat aphids. The strong scent of dill repels the carrot fly so plant dill close to your carrots.
- **Nettles** can be left to flourish in odd corners to attract caterpillars away from brassicas. Then chop down the leaves and add to the compost bin.

See pages 139–147 for more suggestions for good companion plants and how to grow them.

APHIDS

There are many diseases around, mostly spread by aphids—greenfly and blackfly are the most common—so aphid control will help reduce problems.

- Soapy water applied in a hand spray is fairly effective for aphids if applied regularly. Dilute organic washing-up liquid 1:10 in water and spray directly on the pests.
- Spray aphids with a brew of strained rhubarb leaves. Boil up leaves, add a few soap flakes dissolved in warm water, stir and use undiluted as a spray.
- Buy a Lacewing chamber to nail to the shed. Lacewings are insects that prey on aphids. The sturdy wooden box is filled with straw impregnated with a natural pheromone to attract lacewings. They will survive the winter protected in the chamber and be ready to devour all greenfly and blackfly in spring.

SLUGS

- Prevention is best: keep your allotment clean and remove potential slug hiding places.
- Cut the base off a clear plastic bottle and place over young plants until they have reached 10 cm/4 ins. Slugs are more attracted to the smallest leaves.
- After sowing seeds, cover the ground with a length of netting secured with sticks. Leave on until seedlings are 10 cm/4ins, raising it as the leaves grow taller. It stops birds picking out the seeds and inhibits slugs.
- A dish of beer made from a small, shallow container dug in level with the ground and filled to the top will attract and drown slugs. Dot these around and empty and re-fill regularly.
- Trail fine sand or grit alongside your seedlings. Slugs dislike walking over a rough surface.
- Make a small pond by burying a plastic bowl in the ground filled with water. It will attract frogs to devour the slugs.

BIRDS

Small birds such as sparrows can eat emerging seedlings. Tie black button thread to short bamboo canes and run the length of the seedling rows about 5 cm above ground and on either side.

Covering plants with netting will also deter birds, especially pigeons.

MOLES

Moles may be attracted to the earthworms abundant in an organic allotment. Mothballs pushed into their runs may see them off. You may have to seek the help of your local authority if the problem persists.

MICE

Mice love peas and should be deterred with humane mousetraps. You can release the mouse away from your allotment—and other people's!

RABBITS

If rabbits are a problem, you will need to protect the rows with fine chicken wire. This should be at least 1 metre high and sunk another 30 cm below ground.

CONTROLLING COMMON BUGS & DISEASES

Aphids are soft-bodied insects that rapidly cover a plant and feed on the plant juices. The commonest are green, woolly grey or black, and large colonies can appear overnight. Rub them off or spray with a solution of washing-up liquid.

Asparagus beetles will decimate the foliage in one go and then remain in the soil to do the same next spring. Derris powder or liquid usually sees them off.

Blackcurrant gall mite penetrates the flower bud, preventing the fruit from forming. It also carries the virus disease Reversion. Try cutting the plant back to ground level and you should get healthy new growth the following year.

Cabbage white caterpillars may be visible on brassicas and fruit and should be picked off and destroyed. If there are a huge number then spray with salt solution (60g per 4.5litre of water).

Cabbage moth caterpillars can strip the leaves of brassicas in a night. Pick them off and destroy and then spray with derris to kill the larvae.

Cabbage root fly invades the roots of brassicas. They remain in the soil over winter so dig the ground and leave the maggots exposed for the birds. Keep the plot as weed-free as possible as weeds can harbour this particular pest.

Cabbage whitefly appear as clouds of small white insects in summer, but do not do serious damage.

Carrot fly affects carrots, parsnips, celery and parsley. Caused by the larvae of carrot fly feeding on the tissue of the root. Protect with fleece covers.

Celery fly is a tiny fly that lays eggs and the resulting grub tunnels through leaf tissue. Destroy all affected leaves.

Clubroot is a serious fungal disease effecting brassicas. It causes general poor growth in the leaves and distorted roots. It thrives in acid soil, hence the need to lime the soil before planting the cabbage family. Raising the pH level to between 7.2 and 7.5 usually cures the problem and can be done before or after planting.

Downy mildew is a parasitic fungus that sometimes appears if the weather is humid for a long period. Dusty white deposits appear on leaves and stems, and will weaken them if left untreated. Pick off badly affected leaves and burn, then spray with a Bordeaux mixture.

Flea beetle affects radishes and leafy vegetables. The tiny beetle eats holes in leaves and may cause the plant to die. They overwinter in plant debris, so be vigilant and clear away in autumn. Make a trap by coating one side of a piece of wood with thick grease and moving it along the row of plants—the beetles will jump on to it and stick.

Gooseberry sawfly is an insect that can strip the leaves of currant and gooseberry bushes in days. Spray with derris.

Greenfly and **blackfly** are tiny aphids that can smother plants. Put on rubber gloves and rub the aphids off, or spray with derris.

Grey mould is a fuzzy, grey fungal growth known as Botrytis. Clear up dead plant material and provide good air ventilation.

Leaf spot is a fungal disease that may affect peas and broad beans. The spots are brown and look unsightly, but don't usually cause too much damage. Pick off the leaves and put in the refuse bin.

Mosaic virus affects marrows, cucumber, spinach and tomatoes and presents as mottling of the leaves and stunted growth. There is no cure and you will need to lift all infected plants and burn. Greenfly are the main carrier of the disease.

Onion fly is a small grey fly attacking the roots of onions, leeks, garlic and shallots. The first sign is yellowing and dying leaves when the plants are still young. Destroy the plants before they leave maggots in the soil to pupate. These will be visible if you hoe around the roots, and should be put in the refuse bin.

Pea and bean weevil can nibble leaf margins in spring, retarding seedlings. Spray with derris.

Pea moth can attack in summer; the maggot may appear in peas. Grow under fine nets to deter the adult fly, or spray with derris.

Potato eel worms are minute worm-like creatures that attack the roots of potatoes. Destroy all traces of the affected crop, and do not grow on same ground for eight years.

Raspberry beetles feed on the blossom and the larvae burrow into the emerging fruits. Hoe around the base of the canes to expose the pupae to the birds or spray with derris.

Red spider mite leaves small yellow and white markings and webbing on leaves. They attack container-grown plants more than those in the ground. Prevent by keeping container plants well watered.

Reversion is a disease affecting blackcurrants and is indicated by masses of leaf and very little fruit. There is no cure and affected bushes will need to be grubbed out and burnt.

Rust is a fungal disease that presents as yellow spots on the leaves and bright orange or brown spore-bearing pustules underneath. Pick off the affected leaves and destroy.

Thrips are small black insects that lay eggs on peas in mid-summer. A spray with Pyrethrum sees them off.

Tomato and potato blight show as brown marks on leaves with white fungal spores underneath. Remove and destroy all infected leaves. Water the plants at ground level rather than spraying from above. Do not overcrowd at the planting stage; good air circulation is needed for healthy plants.

Violet root rot presents as violet veins covering roots, stems or crowns of plants. The first signs are yellowing leaves and stunted growth, usually in wet, acid soils. Pull up the crop and adjust the pH of the soil before trying again.

Whitefly are small white flies that live on the underside of leaves and fly up in clouds when disturbed. Treat by spraying with organic washing-up liquid diluted with water.

Wireworms live underground and bore holes in carrots and potatoes. They are attracted to wheat, so grow a row of wheat between crops and then dig it up and burn it; or make a decoy with an old potato—bury it, marked with a stick, and then dig it up and burn it. They hide in long grass so once your allotment is fully cultivated they should disappear.

ORGANIC INSECTICIDES & FUNGICIDES

However organic in origin, these should still be used with caution and only after careful analysis of the problem. Follow the manufacturer's instructions and be scrupulous about keeping all products out of reach of children.

Derris is made from the powdered roots of two tropical legumes that contain the insect poison retenone. It is effective against aphids, red spider mite, gooseberry sawfly, asparagus beetle and raspberry beetle. Available as a dust or spray, it has the advantage of being effective for a very short period, such that edible plants can be harvested one day after using it.

Pyrethrum is extracted from *Chyrysanthemum coccineum* and is used against aphids, whitefly, caterpillars, thrips, and beetles. Once diluted it is quickly rendered harmless by sunlight, so that as with derris, crops can be consumed a day later.

Copper fungicide will give excellent control over fungal diseases such as potato blight and tomato leaf mould. Look for Bordeaux or Burgundy Mixtures, and read the labels thoroughly to be sure you are applying the correct one.

Useful Addresses

The following mail order companies offer a wide and unusual range of seeds and seedling plants, many of them organic. Many also supply useful products to help you grow healthy organic produce.

DT Brown & Co Seeds Ltd, Station Road, Poulton-le-Fylde, Lancs FY6 7HX. Tel 0845 6014656 or <www.dtbrownseeds.co.uk>.

Chiltern Seeds, Bortree Stile, Ulverston, Cumbria LA12 7PB. Tel 01229 581137 or <www.chilternseeds.co.uk>.

Mr Fothergill's Seeds, Mail Order Dept., Kentford, Suffolk CB8 7QB. Tel 01638 552512 or <www.mr-fothergills.co.uk>.

Halcyon Seeds, 10 Hampden Close, Chalgrove, Oxford OX44 7SB. Tel 01865 890180 or <www.halcyonseeds.co.uk>.

Jekka's Herb Farm, Rose Cottage, Shellards Lane, Alveston, Nr Bristol BS12 2SY. Tel 01454 418878.

Kings Seeds, Monks Farm, Kelvedon, Colchester, Essex CO5 9PG. Tel 01376 570000 or <www.kingseeds.com>.

Marshalls Seeds (S.E. Marshall & Co Ltd), Freepost PE787, Wisbech, Cambs PE13 2BR. Tel 01945 466711 or <www.marshalls-seeds.co.uk>.

Ken Muir, Honeypot Farm, Rectory Road, Weeley Heath, Essex CO16 9BJ Fruit Supplier Tel 01255 830181.

The Organic Gardening Catalogue, Riverdene Business Park, Molesey Road, Hersham, Surrey KT12 4RG. Tel 01932 253666 or <www.organiccatalog.com>.

Seeds of Italy, 260 West Hendon Broadway, London NW9 6BE. Tel 0208 9302516 or <www.seedsofitaly.com>.

Simpson Seeds, The Walled Garden Nursery, Horningsham, Warminster, Wiltshire BA12 7NQ. Tel 01985 845004 or <www.simpsonseeds.com>.

Suffolk Herbs, Monks Farm, Coggeshall Road, Kelvedon, Essex CO5 9PG. Tel 01376 572456 or <www.suffolkherbs.com>.

Suttons Seeds, Tel 0800 783 8074 or <www.suttons.co.uk>.

Thomson & Morgan Seeds, Poplar Lane, Ipswich, Suffolk IP8 3BU. Tel 01473 688821. <www.thomson-morgan.com>.

Suppliers of Useful Products

Agralan Ltd. The Old Brickyard, Ashton Keynes, Swindon,
Wilts SN6 6QR. Tel 01285 860015. <agralan@cybermail.uk.com>.
Non-chemical pest control, cloches, meshes, fleece and many
products for the allotment.

Dax Products Ltd, PO Box 119, Nottingham NG3 5NA.
Tel 0115 926 9996. Weed control, mulch and landscape products.

Green Gardener, 41 Strumpshaw Road, Brundall, Norfolk NR13 5PG.
Helpline 01603 715096 or Phone/Fax 01603 716986.
<www.greengardener.co.uk>. Biological Control Advice Service.

Plastic Reclamation Ltd, Tel 01744 810001. Boards made from
recycled carrier and bin bags, useful for raised beds.

Pro-Grow Soil Improver, Head Office, CPL Distribution, Mill Lane,
Wingerworth, Chesterfield, Derbyshire, S42 6NG. Tel 0800 328 6693.

H & T Proctor, Phoenix House, 51 Queen Square, Bristol BS1 4LJ.
Tel 0117 311 1217 Supplier of organic fertilizers.

Useful Organizations

The Allotments Regeneration Initiative, The Greenhouse,
Hereford Street, Bristol BS3 4NA. Tel 0117 963 1551.
<www.farmgarden.org.uk/ari>.

Farm and Community Gardens. Tel 0207485 5001
<wwwfarmgarden.or.uk>. A project co-ordinating 160 community
gardens in London where local volunteers grow vegetables and flowers.

Growing Communities. Tel 0207 502 7588. Project organizing
neighbourhood food growing.

Henry Doubleday Research Association (HDRA), Ryton Organic
Gardens, Ryton-on-Dunsmore, Coventry CV8 3LG. Tel 024 7630 3517.

Yalding Gardens, Benover Road, Yalding, Maidstone ME18 6EX.
Tel 01622 814650. A series of organic gardens operated by HDRA
(some vegetable growing) and open to the public.

The National Society of Allotment & Leisure Gardeners,
O'Dell House, Hunters Road, Corby, Northants NN17 5JE.
Tel 01536 266576.

Main Index

Index of Recipes

Also available from Green Books:

HOW TO STORE YOUR GARDEN PRODUCE
Piers Warren

"Entertaining and very practical. A great gift for any gardener."
—*Centre for Alternative Technology*

How to Store Your Garden Produce by organic smallholder Piers Warren shows how to store and preserve your garden produce, enabling you to eat home-grown goodness all year round. The easy to use reference section enables you to quickly look up applicable storage and preservation techniques for the majority of plant produce grown commonly in gardens and allotments. The techniques include • freezing • clamping • hanging • drying • bottling • pickling • and fermenting. ISBN 1 903998 25 5 **£4.95 paperback**

BACKYARD COMPOSTING
John Roulac

Composting at home reduces your personal volume of rubbish, conserves water, increases plant growth, replaces the need for toxic chemical fertilizers and pesticides, and is also fun. Backyard Composting also introduces the various types of composting bins and accessories, explaining the pros and cons of each type, and gives instructions for building one from scrap materials. ISBN 1 900322 11 0 **£4.95 paperback**

LIQUID GOLD
The Lore and Logic of Using Urine to Grow Plants
Carol Steinfeld

Don't flush it down the loo—save your pee and fertilize your garden! Because it is not recycled, our urine is wasted and pollutes the water system. Yet it could provide 50%–100% of the nutrients needed to grow our food. Use your pee to make a liquid manure: recycle, save water and energy, and prevent pollution, all at the same time! Discover the delights of the urine-diverting composting toilet and the urinal for women; find out about customs and rituals connected with urine, the science and technology of its use, and profiles of liquid gold at work all over the world in farms and gardens. Fertilize your garden for free with Carol Steinfeld's entertaining and fact-filled book! ISBN 1 903998 48 4 **£4.95 paperback**

*and many more books on ecological living including
eco-building, food, lifestyle, literature and travel.*

*For our latest catalogue phone 01803 863260,
or visit our website: www.greenbooks.co.uk*